The Escape Artists

Ben Parker

THE ESCAPE ARTISTS

ISBN – 13: 978 - 1 - 904551 - 86 - 7

A CIP record for this title is available from the British Library.

Published by tall-lighthouse press.

ACKNOWLEDGEMENTS

My thanks to the editors of the following publications, where some of these poems originally appeared or are forthcoming: Anon, Body, Eunoia Review, Fourteen, Fuselit, Ink Sweat & Tears, The Journal, Lung Jazz, Oxford Poetry, Popshot.

Special thanks are due to all those who have offered feedback on these poems, and to my family for their continued support.

Back Cover Photograph by David Jones

CONTENTS

Do you remember that day we found the first horse? It was skittering the dust in a forgotten field adjacent to a farmhouse that must have stood forever if not longer. This was the horse from which all other horses were bred; the horse of cave-paintings and untranslatable mythology. Undomesticated, rough-haired, and small, it looked more like a mongrel dog. We took it to the backyard of our rented ground-floor flat. Our friends came over to see it. That's a dog, they told us. We resolved not to speak to them again. We brought our horse fresh-cut grass every spring and oats throughout the winter but it grew thin and restless. We asked your uncle, the vet, to inspect it for us. He took you into a corner and spoke in a gentle concerned tone, as though he had forgotten you were an adult. You sent him away and cried for a bit. That evening, to cheer you up, we watched a documentary on horses and thought how proud our horse must be to have delivered this noble race. Do you remember that day we found the first horse chewing a rubber ball thrown over by the neighbours?

Sideshow

The circus itches. Pipes play on
though there is no-one around to hear them.
The bones of candyfloss point the way
past the halted carousel and empty mirrors.
My appointment was two hours ago
if the fortune cookie is to be believed
but without knowing which of my services
is required it is hard to choose
from among the shrouded cages.
Licked sticks proliferate and I tread
the same giant discarded cartoon dog
deeper into mud. The tents are talking to me.
The strong-man sleeps in a fug of beer,
the dwarves dream of Hollywood,
and I will still be here when dawn breaks.
Gather round! Watch as he checks a map
he doesn't have, see him turn on the spot
in the same exact place night after night,
and from this tower, madam, marvel
as he spells his own name eight-feet high
with his footprints, The Amazing Lost Man!

The Path

Near my old ancestral home is a village
at whose tree-lined edge

a path begins
which doesn't end

until it reaches the corner
of the horn of Africa

and dries up on a beach.
Its reach

requires that it twice slide into the ocean
with no more concern

than when a car dips
into a valley filled with mist

emerging with its lights still lit
the bonnet wet

and the passengers none the wiser
at the next rise.

It is only as wide
as two horses side by side

and thin
from many months of walking.

House of Rivers

For days you hear the din of wind
through trees as simply that, until
your fire hangs a cord of smoke
from the sky, straight as a plumb-line,
and your finger comes down damp
with the lick you planted on it still warm
and you know that you are close. Two hours
and you are facing the house. By now
the sound has grown so loud
it seems that all the rivers of the world
have burst their banks to run as one.
The walls are unscrolling from the roof
and going to ground in broken waves;
the door stands open centre left,
as though a rock or fallen branch
has blocked the water's path.
The earth tips back to point at dusk
and sun shines clear through the frame
lighting the unobstructed stream
bending unbidden round the lintel.
You dip your head to step inside.
Within an hour your skin is bloated;
after two you no longer blink
at the spray coughed in your face.
By morning your lungs have shrunk
to stones; your neck flares as you breathe.

DIY

On the day she left he hung the final mirror,
filling the space where the front door was
and facing inwards. Not a surface remained
that didn't affirm the infinite regression
of itself. He walked from room to room
and knew, if nothing else, that he was there.
Only the real exists in such profusion.

Now the lighting of a match is a universe
jolted into time; each reflected sulphur-flare
a momentary blinding, burning its quick term
and fading to smoky dark. One bare lamp
is enough to illuminate his house, the true source
never found by any moth, drawn as they are instead
to that first encountered insufficient glare.

The Lake

There is a lake that freezes
once only in a lifetime. The centre
holds an island, squat as a bronze boss
on a silver shimmering shield, too distant
to be seen from shore although the lake
is small and could be shouted over
on a day when the wind is right.
It is miles from the nearest village,
shaded from the sun by a neat
half-moon of craggy, treeless mountains
and is a place you would not visit twice.
But come when weather warnings
have cleared the paths of weekend walkers
and all the native birds have passed you
on their journey south and you might find
the water fastened down with ice.
And if you choose to make the walk
don't stop. The surface creaks
and mutters at your back. Speed up,
keep the looming island in your sight.
The freeze will hold you only once.

From the Histories I

Conflicting reports were delivered daily
from the city of high walls and no gates.
The crops were flourishing even
as the wells came up dry. Rebellion
chattered in the streets, which weekly
filled with impromptu festivals
in the emperor's honour. His statues
were decked with tributes, songs
echoed with his name and the one
image of his true likeness had its
eyes painted black and the frame
abused in diverse strange manners.
We believed the worst, supposing
the rest propaganda, and yet no-one
tried to leave that city, while our sons
and daughters set off to attempt entry.
From those who were successful
we heard only of wonders: that wine
was drained directly from fruit still
hung on the branch, the rivers ran
with fat and docile fish, and the gods
walked the markets, selling charms
for a low price and without obligation.

The Way

Drive again through the last outlying
rain-shuttered village, beyond
the final fuel stop, past where the road inclines,
inclines again, then levels out.
Tune the radio to the dead melodies
of that country's only great composer
and focus on the dwindling road ahead.
As you move outside the station's reach
wait for the rising background static
to mingle with the trumpet's sombre melody
and when the closing note
is lost beneath that black scrawl
crank the volume dial clockwise
drop your windows, let your car become
a needle in a groove of infinite diameter.
That sound is not the shifting of the continents,
not the heaving of the gathered clouds
or stretching of the oak's dark roots.
That sound is not your lover's breath
but tonight it's near enough.

Remembrances
for K.J.

A silver ring by the kitchen sink, your dress
embracing my jacket on the rail,
and on the floor those intimate blacks and reds
like crumpled flowers, lying where they fell.

By these tokens, and others, you let me know
forgetful as you are, you will return.
No sooner has the door clicked to
than I begin my search from room to room.

Painting Your Voice

Not the actual words, you understand,
merely the shape your breath makes
when speaking, the way your tongue
works as a chisel on your sentences.

Perhaps the paint they use on gates,
the type that never dries, would work.
If I could stand at your side while you talk
in a room where the air is perfectly still.

Watch. Like smoke caught in a breeze
a contrail leads from the paintbrush
loaded at your lips to the whitewashed
opposite wall and leaves its mark.

Now let's step outside and find a hill
where the wind blows fiercely west
and let it take your speech and send it
like papers flung towards the sea.

Your voice is blossom on the ocean
carried by the tides to other shores,
other listeners. The heat will lift it up
and over mountains it will fall as rain.

Church Flatts Farm

All night the waves are in his room
lifting him from half-dreams
of bladder-wrack and drift-wood.
The walls breathe like filling sails,
the blood-tide beats in his ears.
He is feverish and sleepless, far
from instruments, with no navigator
and the Pole Star lost behind plaster.

When arthritis closed around his hands
he left the sea and made his way here,
the furthest he could move inland,
and stripped his boat to make a bed.
Mornings now he wakes with dry lips,
salt-blur glazing the window.

The Restaurant

I

Most of the walls are black with the juice
of berries imported for just that purpose.
On those not daubed with the dark liquid
hang candid photos of your distant relatives
committing petty and archaic crimes.

II

The waiters are dressed for a funeral
and the concierge questions your levity
in the face of such grief. You are handed
 a wine-list bound with the hair of every
beautiful woman who has ever dined there.

III

On entering, the lights are turned so high
you can feel the heat falling from them.
Within minutes the smell of sweating cheese
and humid fish has filled the dining area.
The windows and doors are sealed for effect.

IV

In place of menus are books of ingredients
subdivided into three independent segments,
such as are used by children to construct
chimeras. Someone has substituted one panel
of the main courses with one from the desserts.

V

The entire restaurant, including kitchen,
has been moved into the toilets while
'renovations' take place. On entering,
all parties are segregated by sex.
You may help yourself to the tap-water.

VI

A week before dining you must submit portraits
and brief summaries of friends with whom
you have lost touch. When you arrive the cooks
are wearing masks depicting your friends' faces
and mimic their mannerisms with absurd exaggeration.

VII

Sensitive microphones have been fixed
under some of the tables and the sounds
are relayed instantly to speakers set at a volume
just high enough to be heard. Today the first hints
of feedback are creeping into the layered chatter.

Storm Line

Even before you call, it broods behind the earpiece,
a fidget of pressure shifting under the static. Punch
the code into the beige of the handset and sudden
turbulence will threaten to crush the phone
in your hand. Speak and the storm will answer.
Stay silent and for as long as you are on the line
lightning will sear the sky with the din of the bolt,
the rip of the unleashed charge.

And even if you don't know the number, listen
to the hum of the dial tone as you call a friend,
to the gap between urgent chimes as your phone
jolts awake when no-one knows you're in.
You will hear the thunder's distant argument, rain
muttering dissent. The wind raising its voice.

18

First Inhabitant of the Asylum

At times she simply stands for days
in front of windows smeared with rain;
others, drawn on a cord of hunger,
she turns towards the strip-lit kitchen
for a tin of soup or beans that someone
must have taught her to open
but not to cook: the hob snug
in polythene, the drawer of spoons
sealed shut, kettle and toaster unplugged.
Through the endless rise and fall of years
she keeps her frail clockwork turning.
The wren that darts from a bush is
as nameless to her as the fists in her pockets;
the stacks of clouds that perform daily
are just shapes against a changing wall.
Trees shiver and tap the glass,
rusted heat-pipes grumble,
and she drags her feet in sterile corridors
waiting for the rest of them to arrive.

Day's Last Wave

Each afternoon he would make the drive
15 miles west from his house to see
the breaking of the last wave of the day.
Armed with an accurate prediction
of the time of its setting, and with
one eye on the sun (or if obscured
by a cloud, on the second-display
of his digital waterproof watch)
the other on the lick of the surf
as it ran along the parched lip
of this small secluded gravel beach.
As the end of the sun teased the edge
of the horizon he would prepare
to record the details of the final wave
unfolding in daylight, noting down
in his third thick notebook the sound
as it sprawled against the stones, the height,
approximately, before it fell
and the colours of its collapsing body.
When he arrived home he could still hear
the push and sigh of the sea working
at the shore in the thickening dark.

Heroine's Bath (after Daniel Eltinger)

She sees a kingfisher's wing
and a lizard's pupil set in shining skin;

the nacreous glaze on the dinner plates,
the fish heads, pheasant, candied dates,

the children at their games,
wine on the carpet, flames.

Mid-day breaking through the thin guise
of her drowsy, half-closed eyes,

then the darkening sky above her head,
and stars against the last of sunset's red.

She sees the gathered dust
on her late father's copper bust;

his robes of state and the graveyard trees
stirred by a cold unwelcome breeze.

She sees the blue porcelain, and the water
as it fills with the life of no-one's daughter.

One Place

Out here the elms echo with the eagle-shout
and sparrow-cry; leaves tune the wind;
the only path is the one your trespass cuts.

Your car is waiting at the forest's edge
with autumn already falling on its roof.
You bag and bury your mud clad-shoes

before rejoining the nightly homeward grind,
just another commuter locked to a private frequency.
Delay can be explained by deadlines,

accidents or (at a push) affairs. Your wife
would sooner sanction a sexual betrayal
than bless your return here,

the one place still forbidden to you both.

The Escape Artists

Drop them on a cracked and shifting terminal planet and watch them sink into the death-fog. Mineral deposits low, gravity failing, and there ain't room on the periodic table for the shit cooking down there. Watch them sink into the end-boil.

Roll up, roll up and see the two black body-suits drill their way to the core, through the chemical churn and kinetic noise of total decay, as the feedback scream of overloaded instruments ties the readout graphs in senseless knots. A thousand screens blaze a thousand annotated views of the distant shredded globe as it begins its final orbit, the decisive cycle before the Split, before a million rock-spores spin off from the dust of another finished world. This is the part of the show they call The Wait: Pure entertainment ladies and gentlemen! Introspection ad nauseum elevated to art! Hear the roar of nothing! Think you've been expectant before? Think you know how to deal with delay? Welcome to The Wait! Seen it already you say? They always return? Ask yourself this though...can you be sure?

This is the only true silence. The sound-absence framed by the ear-burn of super volume. Off the scale volume. One millionth of a decimal place below maximum volume. But the deficit has the monopoly on this one. Listen to its howl. This is the silence the Escape Artists surf, the held-breath multi-hour gap between vanishing and resurgence. This is the birth-gap. The forever-wait until eternity becomes mortality. A million upturned faces watch again and again. This is a trick that never gets old. Every time those two sleek forms rip from the pull, trailing the last gasps of atmosphere in their wake, every time the graphics jump into life announcing blood-pressure, body-heat, hydration-levels, pupil-dilation, mass, height, pulse, and every time the deep-sphere vid-pics flash-up, we see once more our conception, our delivery, our struggle from death to being and back.

Cinema of the Drowned

Suspended behind the swollen screen
and held in place by a horizontal trick
of surface tension, bodies shift
in the creak and groan of the straining deep:
limbs curved in careless abandon as though
subsiding at the apex of a jump,
hair swept by the flex of the current.
Once again you pass the hidden entrance,
walk on, change your mind, turn back and enter,
picking your way through the empty seats
in the mute dark far from the crest
and trough of the waves. Sit back and bathe
in the cold glow of sea-filtered moonlight,
the grey saturated flesh of the dead.
The seat is warm from your last visit,
listen: you still cannot fathom the drag.

From the Histories II

The Shogun's palace is surrounded
by a field of bells that always ring,
strung as they are on light ankle-high
wooden frames, designed to catch
the famous breeze lifting from the valley
and fanning constantly the open
courtyards and surrounding landscape
of this magnificent ancient dwelling.
So familiar is the movement of the air
to the Shogun, so deeply lodged
in the bloodline its seasonal changes
and daily agitations, that the orchestrated
music is as predictable to him
as his own heartbeat, and any disturbance
could indicate the advance of assassins
who, well-trained though they are
in the art of silent approach, cannot hear
an individual bell ring out of time
above the din. Even in drunken sleep
the Shogun knows when the tune is wrong
and wakes to dispatch his guards.
Thus his reign continues, and his family
will glorify the earth with their presence
for a thousand years, while their wives
and daughters stuff their ears with wax
and develop the intricate sign-language
for which their line is justly remembered.

ne

The day that didn't happen

"Soon I could conceal the secret so well that I could smile straight at him. As though nothing had happened, or as though it didn't have anything to do with me at all – as though I had nothing to hide, it was all assimilated. As though the day hadn't happened."

A small Norwegian town in August 1975. A heatwave. A 12-year-old girl, who is no longer a child. An incident that no one must know about. A dark secret – and an extraordinary love story.

Gerd Kvanvig was born in 1965 and grew up in Jessheim, near Oslo. Having decided that her future lay in writing rather than ballet, she made her literary debut in 1994 with a poetry collection called *Persona*. She has since published five novels in Norwegian, all written in her distinctly lyrical style: *The Extraordinary Heart* (1995), *Paradise Entered* (1999), *The day that didn't happen* (2000), *The Murderer's Tale* (2009) and *Messages from the Death Planet* (2010). As well as being an author, Gerd Kvanvig teaches Norwegian at Jessheim Upper Secondary School. She now lives in Oslo.

Also by Gerd Kvanvig

Poetry
Persona, Cappelen, 1994

Novels
Det ekstraordinære hjertet, Cappelen, 1995
Paradiset innskrevet, Tiden Norsk Forlag, 1999
Dagen som ikke finnes, Tiden Norsk Forlag, 2000
Morderens fortelling, Forlaget Oktober, 2009
Meldinger fra dødskloden, Forlaget Oktober, 2010

The day that didn't happen

Gerd Kvanvig

translated by *Wendy H. Gabrielsen*

Naked Eye Publishing

First published in the Norwegian language as
'Dagen som ikke finnes' by Gerd Kvanvig (Tiden norsk Forlag,
2000)

First published in English translation
by Naked Eye Publishing 2022

This translation has been published with the financial
support of NORLA

NORLA
Norwegian
Literature
Abroad

Book design, typesetting and front cover by Naked Eye

ISBN: 9781910981221

nakedeyepublishing.co.uk

Translator's acknowledgements

I would like to thank Mum and Stein for being my first readers, and Gerd, Mike and NORLA for giving me my first break in the UK.

The day that didn't happen

His grasp around my wrist is unyielding.

His eyes are empty.

And when he has me up close to him, I feel an enormous pressure building in my lungs – and the transition from fear to greater fear makes room for a further transition. Fear is a raging force.

There's a pressure coming from a place so deep in my lungs that the world is confirmed as impossibly huge in a collision between us. Everything is reduced to fear – but the fear is endless.

I am furious, I kick, bite, hit.

He's wearing a vest, his shoulders are bare, and he's holding a knife against my face. Against my cheek. A slight pressure of metal against skin.

The tip of the knife is in front of my eye – and he's angry, and I've suddenly always known that it's possible to be so angry.

His breath drags over my lips. His face has changed from tenderness to fury, it rubs against my body while the knife is like a cut already, against my neck. And then he grabs me differently, tugs my head back by my ponytail, places his mouth over my stomach and gives it a wet bite.

Every summer when I was small, there was a funfair and market on the field between the town hall and the railway station in Jessheim. It was called the Jessheim Festival. One weekend in August, the shops would move out into market stalls. There was a funfair and candyfloss and useful and useless things for sale – great stuff for children. There was an atmosphere of innocent excitement and commotion. The people that travelled with the fair came from far away and were wonderfully exotic. The afternoons were golden and the evenings bright blue.

On the Saturday there was a concert and a dance. And the year I turned twelve the group that had won the Eurovision Song Contest came, the ones that sang "Ding-a-Dong", so sharp-edged and melancholy.

I sat by the balcony door of our flat with the radio on. Up the road in Jessheim I knew they were putting up the fair. It was morning, no wind at all. The sun looked like it had burst and covered the whole sky. Everything was lit up by white-hot sun. Inside, the shadows were extra dark, but they too were filled with the sun's warmth. Just the concrete walls still gave off a faint chill, and moisture steamed from the laundry I had hung up on the balcony.

The music on the radio was the only thing that was really clear. Music was rooted in me. I turned off the radio, walked through the dark sitting room into the hall and slipped on my clogs, jamming my feet into them just inside the front door where I had kicked them off on the way in. I pulled the door shut behind me, skipped down the stairs one at a time, one leg at a time, down the three floors and out.

Outside, the sun burnt into my skin. I didn't have sunglasses or sun lotion. Just the key around my neck. I was wearing an old yellow towelling summer dress. We called it a sundress. It was like a veil, it was so threadbare. I had hardly worn anything else the whole summer and it was second hand when I got it, and now it billowed like a threadbare veil. I grabbed my bike, which was leaning against the wall, breathed in the cool and up-close air of the shade where all movements for miles around could be read on the skin, and cycled at great speed up to Jessheim.

I stopped at "Fruity" and bought an ice lolly. Then I stood with the bike between my legs, licking the lolly while I watched the newly arrived fairground workers assembling structures and stalls, carrying steel pipes and large boards, smoking, walking back and forth, in a pattern, a game that I didn't know but immediately understood. A word here and there, laughter.

I was still on my way as I stood there watching, along with the other kids roaming around the place – small bees encircling the heavy sweetness of things going on, of change and unfamiliarity.

The cars that droned past on the busy road, whirling up dry grit and dust, the train from town that eased heavily into the station, mothers with children in prams on their way to and from the shops, teenagers on their bikes laughing loudly, on their way to Nordby lake with their swimming things, the conductor that blew his whistle for departure, waving a green flag – all sounds and movements were an integral part of the burst sunlight.

It was the middle of August 1975, the year I turned twelve, and there was something about the night air too – it was something I realised at the time. Something at once beautiful, hellish and nothing. And I don't understand what it is. But I know what it is. There's something about the night air of late summer, the way it is mine, and me, and not at all. It's just a feeling; even so, this feeling has affected my whole life, and it might be this – whatever it is – that made me survive what happened.

There's something about the structure of open, night-blue August skies in me.

Sun-blue hot nights.

A chilly haze of greenish-white drizzle for weeks afterwards. Large icy drops of early autumn rain on a day in September.

There's something about this kind of connection between me and the weather that has gained a symbolic status, that captures what has been so decisive for my life, that has meant I have led the life I have led (I'm quite sure about this) – but I still don't know what it is.

I was twelve, it was the year I had turned twelve in May, and the group that won the Eurovision Song Contest with "Ding-a-Dong" played at the Jessheim Festival, and it seems impossible to say what happened. Impossible just to remember.

It is still this August light that forms the basis of the incident. A temperature. Breath. Nothing. And yet it seems to be this nothing between me and the rhythm of light and wind and earth that can make the incident clear, and possible to talk about.

The cobalt blue afternoons of nothing that keep seeping back in colours and shapes.

The smell of rain and earth in September, wet, rotting grass. Half-melted rime in a sudden delay of warmth …

The grass outside our block of flats was scorched that day in August when the funfair came – the grass on the side of the building where there wasn't shade and where people stomped back and forth, and at the playground and places where there wasn't a proper lawn, at the side of the roads, by the walls.

The grass on the other side, towards the west, under the balconies, in the shade cast by the neighbouring blocks of flats – that was still lush and green. A refreshing relief, a weighty damp. I sat in the shade tearing up thick, green grass, I let it run through my fingers and gathered it into small, cool bird's nests of grass (even though I was too old for that sort of thing). I breathed as if through a miniscule filter, taking breaths of sprouting life.

Finally, I put all the grass into a small, faded bucket that had spent the winter under the bottom balcony and made a nest that I hid under the stairs down in the lobby. I placed a round, smooth stone inside.

It was late morning and quiet. Almost no cars. Mum was asleep. People walked slowly back and forth, as if suspended between sun and sun. Kids hung around in small groups, in pairs, on bikes. A few by themselves. Almost everyone had come back from their holidays, as school was about to start. An old woman from Brinken had been shopping and was walking back down the road again in slow motion. Breathing heavily.

All the sounds were distant pulses – but light, light and slow ripples of life through the heat.

I sat at the bottom of the stairs with the grass nest behind me, behind stone and concrete and steps. The door was open, and the opening was a sun-mirror. Outside, the air vibrated with sharp, static waves of light. The ding-ding song about flowers and lovers continued in the background.

And I played "The Boxer" by Simon and Garfunkel again and again on Erling's cassette player all that autumn. And survived.

And now it might seem as if I'm establishing a link, like a cause and effect, between music and survival. Perhaps I am. I don't know – but it's as if this nothing that was so significant at that time (and still is) has the structure of music's hold on me. Something like that.

It was August-hot, August-cold, a fat bud, so strong, so soft, so rotten-ripe. Exactly like that.

It was the hottest summer since 1959, and it didn't rain until the end of August.

The week following the Jessheim Festival, it began to rain. Monday 18 August. It was the first day of school after the holidays, and I was starting class 6.

It was like looking into the future the whole time – living acutely. And everything was clear in a fierce blow of knowledge, about what was possible. But of course I couldn't have known what was going to happen that August night in 1975, no more than it's possible for a twelve-year-old to look further back than twelve years into the past.

And yet – I saw Grandad's face far back in time.

When he laughed as he leant on his axe, bending over to pick up the firewood he'd chopped, I could see his smooth face from the wedding photo of him and Granny. When he laughed leaning over to throw the firewood into the woodshed with the other firewood and logs, and only just concealed a smile as he looked at me and saw himself as the youngster he had once been, his childhood self.

Did he look like me? A young man who had ended up on a little farm in Romerike and become old and twisted, but remained unchanged, he looked like me.

And I saw him even further back in time, I saw him reminiscing when he caught my eye. Just a moment, but it was definitive. And it still resonates.

Each wrinkle's calmness a measure of how to keep facing the world.

He spoke slowly and in detail, concentrating, almost intensely, and with a clear intention that the stories he told would reach a space inside me, not the other way round. This is how he spoke, not so that I had to enter his narrative space, but so that we could share it. In the woodshed. At the kitchen table covered with a faded plastic cloth, where I sat afterwards while he continued working. The sunlight portioned out, in through the windows in trembling patches of light over white, orderly window ledges, over the faded plastic tablecloth with vague flower patterns, over the floorboards. Light through a glass that made time not pass, but come. I sat there watching the patches of sunlight move and gradually disappear, the light still moving, trembling, inside me too, forever afterwards.

In the same way, it was as if I knew exactly what could happen that August day in 1975 – knew before it happened. The feelings were so vague and open that the possibility was clear in the naked gaze, a gaze without prejudice of any kind, and that nonetheless is derived from and balanced in all acquired knowledge. Where anything can happen. A gaze balanced through to the place inside where everything that encounters senses and thoughts is engraved, naked and exposed, and delivers a report. True.

And when I walk through the grass I smelt at the time – dry, freshly mown, wet – I shall sit next to myself, in the wind. And when I turn around and look back, I shall smooth down my hair – because it isn't me, it isn't my hands, it's hands of wind, water, nothing – and I shall look forward to something else, something more.

And it's my hands after all. That's how it was. It was me.

Cold grass at night, for instance. The smell of sprouting and mute life. I smell it right through, I am drenched with cold-mown grass at night and still something is piercingly more than vegetation and rhythms of light and water.

I would sit at the bottom of the stairs when Mum went to work. Then it was my job to go inside the flat. When it got dark.

I wasn't afraid of the dark outside, but inside the flat the dark outside was directed at me, or so it seemed. Inside the flat, the dark was locked in and I couldn't escape it. The inside dark wasn't my dark. Sometimes I would sit in the armchair in front of the TV, in the corner, until the last programme ended. Sitting there unable to move. I'd fall asleep like that. Wake up with a jolt and run to my bed, sit in the innermost corner of the bed in the innermost corner of the flat and listen, keeping an eye on things. I listened so intently that I felt the static heartbeats in everything outside, from the other side, in my breath. And back again. The cars on the motorway, the train hurtling past behind the forest of fir trees, someone banging on a door in the building, voices on the road outside. The sound of the silence between, where everything begins. I sat stiffly and kept watch, until I fell asleep from exhaustion.

Even as a child I knew that I looked just like my mother, that we had the same grey eyes, that I would probably come to resemble her. A long, lanky body with big hands. Inclined to get dry skin, wrinkles. Ugly but with strength. Anything else?

Margrete. My name felt strangely out of place. I used to think, no, maybe I only felt it – in any case, I had a complete yet fragile feeling that it was a kind of miracle I was called Margrete. The name reached out to other worlds, my world.

When Queen Margrete of Denmark got married, I was four and stood in the doorway between the kitchen and sitting room at Grandad's watching them watch the wedding. Granny was still alive then, but I don't remember her. I remember that the queen was on TV and they commented on how splendid she looked, and I said (according to Grandad): "I'm Margrete Splendid," as splendid wasn't a word we used in my family, and I probably thought it meant something else. I don't know. What I remember is that they laughed at me. And I think it's the only memory I have of Mum laughing. A kind of memory.

Mum was at work that night, Saturday 16 August. She was subjected to a staunch-stiff rhythm at its most relentless. And she had got to the point where she didn't even say what I was and wasn't allowed to do. It was at any rate obvious that I was supposed to keep everything clean, make my tea when I came in from school, and not to wake her before four.

It's still not clear to me today what she actually did. Of course I know she was a nurse, but I could never picture it, and still can't, not really, I can't picture what she did…

Maybe it's because the only way she showed that she cared was in the material sense. She provided an income. But she also so clearly mourned the absence of kind words and everyday attentions. She seemed powerless faced with the flat's emptiness, her own flat. She grieved over her evasive glances and lack of intimacy. But the grief itself was exhausted, or never existed, unconceived in an unseeing joylessness. And it's so sad that this image – Mum in her nurse's uniform, white coat – this resembles the memory of the unspeakable thing that happened. Both are somewhat clear and distinct, it's not that there aren't words for it, but it's impossible to understand. No, actually, it's understandable, but impossible to grasp, and embrace. It's impossible to recall in other than unpleasant, uncontrolled glimpses. But to remember is to embrace, I have learnt. And to remember properly, not to overlook significant things, you must forget. You must cut out the memory and embrace it in one single movement. And in that paradox the world comes into view.

With the dusk the heat eased a bit, became rounder, separate, tangible. I sat on the balcony floor, out of sight, watching the sunlight sink into the dense forest of fir trees in the west. And when the heat cooled down and became separate, it also became closer, and I needed it even more in a way, as though something else was about to give. But the heat was mine, always, I owned it. The light was mine through the night.

It was Saturday.

I had watched children's TV, *The Summer on Mirabell Island*, and done the washing up. And then there was that feeling I had, cycling up to Jessheim in the evening after we had watched the news and Mum had gone to work. It was the feeling I had while I was up there, while I floated around and around the fairground, the closed market stalls. Among strangers. And it was the same feeling that saw me home afterwards – a pure structure of cycling, speed, breeze. That was what guided me inside and into the bathtub and out again, down under the stairs.

Afterwards I sat under the stairs. That was where I started sitting when I had to be alone. When it had become impossible to do anything else.

The four white three-storey blocks of flats at Brinken. The only real blocks of flats in Jessheim in those days. Made of concrete. With black, matt-painted window frames.

We lived in the one nearest the woods, by the car park and the school. All the buildings smelt of dry Leca concrete and damp plaster. The stairway was wide, not at all ornate. A dark wooden rail and steps made of stone. The outside doors were insubstantial.

When I was younger I used to sit on the bottom step, but after what happened I sat under the stairs, where no one could see me. It was both a kind of no-place and my own place.

I don't know how Erling found me there. Maybe he heard me, maybe I sat there whimpering.

I just remember that I sat there holding my breath until I felt sick and my tongue dried in my mouth. I couldn't move. I was wide awake. My heart was pounding incredibly fast, and just went on and on. Until day broke, and I started to let go, breathe out, nod off. Then the door opened, and my heart started pounding again. Someone went quickly up the stairs, the door slammed shut again – and I dared to look up.

It was morning and I ran up the stairs and into the flat. Got into bed.

It was Sunday, the day after. I lay there thinking what illness I should feign. *I feel sick and keep throwing up.* That was what happened – the nausea and vomiting from the night before hadn't gone away, I decided. Because that's what can happen.

That's what happened. And I fell deeply asleep. Didn't hear Mum come home.

The next day she was extra quiet, thankfully. She didn't ask too much about the nausea. Said nothing. I lay in bed, alert. Read an old Donald Duck comic. Sat stiffly by the window looking at the forest, the moving cars.

The next day school started.

I sat by the window on the morning school started, unable to move. I sat watching Johanne and her sisters walk past on their way to school. But I just knew I had to stay home. That's how it had to be. It was obvious.

It rained – big, sodden raindrops that fell silently and became a floating slice of hazy glass against green woods and grey sky. I sat with my forehead against the windowpane looking through the rain, sucking in its sound. The sound of the world through the rain, plops of rain on shoulders, against walls, splashes from cars driving through puddles.

Mum had gone straight to sleep when she got home on Monday morning and didn't realise that I hadn't gone to school.

Sometimes she wasn't already asleep when I left in the morning. She would wander around in her dressing gown, go to the loo, have a glass of water in the kitchen, or call out for me, through the flat. *Margrete, is that you? Are you there, Margrete?*

I sat by the window in my room preparing myself in case Mum woke up that Monday, and maybe asked how it had been at school. My first day back at school.

That was when I saw Erling for the first time, the policeman we knew was going to move into the flat across the hallway.

Someone came and parked their car in our parking space.

It was him. I knew straight away.

He was light on his feet, suntanned, and had brown hair. I don't know … It was the way he held his head, how he looked straight in front of him, and just let things be. He made everything different and yet everything was as before. It was the way he moved … He was wearing dark suit trousers and his white shirt sleeves were rolled up over the elbow. He loosened his tie as he shut the car door and started to walk toward the flats; he turned his head, as if he was loosening that too, while he moved, both determined and relaxed. Dragged one leg slightly. And he smiled, or so it seemed, even though he was by himself.

He was carrying a dark grey ring file, not in his hand, but under his arm, along with his suit jacket. In his hand he held a newspaper.

That's how I saw him. I don't know if that's how he came that morning. But that was how I saw him for the first time. He was quite young, but he reminded me of Grandad. There was something about the way he walked, the way he looked up at my window, noticed he was being watched. Heavy and agile at the same time, that's how he was. I quickly moved away from the window, but it was too late, he had seen me.

◊ ◊ ◊

"Margrete, did you know I'm the world champion at making cocoa?"

At first I smiled because Erling was trying to make me smile, because I realised that was what he wanted me to do, because I had to pretend there was nothing wrong, and because I saw that he was struggling too, to reach me.

It was like turning on a light switch – and suddenly not only was what had happened switched off, but now not even the act of secrecy was any longer my act. It couldn't be mine; it too had to sink into an interval that was out of touch with the world. For it was me. Secrecy had to sink into me somewhere, somewhere I wasn't in touch with the world.

"My name's Erling," he said.

I tried to smile.

"What's your name?" he asked.

I can't remember if I answered. But I smiled faintly.

But I didn't smile properly yet, because secrecy was still partly ingrained in my muscles. I looked straight at Erling with a seemingly shy smile, for I still had something to hide.

It wasn't the incident itself I had to hide, that was switched off. *That* was me. But the act of forgetting was still apparent in my face, as I switched it off – and smiled lopsidedly, thirsting for help.

Soon I could conceal the secret so well that I could smile straight at him. As though nothing had happened, or as though it didn't have anything to do with me at all – as though I had nothing to hide, it was all assimilated. As though the day hadn't happened.

Because I hid it so well? I didn't suppress it. It wasn't that the incident had disappeared from my memory. But it was as if it had been cut out of me, had happened ages ago. And this was a surgical process that comprised all my interactions with the world. I sat motionless for hours. Unconscious yet awake. As if I had to stop moving to be able to move again. I noticed when it came, like a storm in reverse. I would go and sit under the stairs, and stay there. Hiding.

I don't know what would have happened if Erling hadn't found me asleep, sitting stiffly under the stairs again early in the morning of the second day of school. I sat there asleep.

Perhaps I would have stayed there? Forever. Perhaps I would have gone back up and made cocoa myself? Perhaps a sound, perhaps someone that came down the stairs and slammed the door, letting fresh morning rain in, would have pulled me out of my trance. Perhaps I would have worn of my own accord the smile that meant nothing had happened … But it seems impossible – that I could have managed it alone, to get up and leave. It feels like I would have sat there forever, never moved on, never gone to school, if Erling hadn't come. I would have stayed sitting inside myself, at least. Stuck.

It was as though the burden of what had happened, when he saw me sitting there like that and silently understood, was shared with him. An ultimate secret kept in pure closeness, and pure distance.

He was the one who drove me on, who held me tight through the air, with his thoughts, his presence. I'm sure it was his presence that made it possible in the years after for me to gradually, gradually become intimate with others' skin without fear, open up for the forces between skin and skin, grasp …

"It's true, I'm the world champion at making cocoa. Didn't you watch the cocoa world cup in Vienna? Of course you did. Would you like some? With cream? Without cream? Whipped cream with stiff peaks? Soft peaks? The consistency of the cream is extremely important, you know. It's one of the things that make all the difference …"

He gave me quick and intense glances when I sat at his kitchen table for the first time. He moved nimbly between the work surface and oven, cups, cocoa, milk and saucepan. As if everything depended on the cocoa.

And I nodded with my lips pressed together and a tiny

smile. I was still stiff, and seemingly shy.

"Grandad's dead," I said.

◊ ◊ ◊

Something happened when Grandad died the year before, in September 1974. I was eleven.

Before he died, I always used to go there at the weekend. Every weekend, and every holiday.

And this thrill over the light and smell of August and September, the weather and changes – wasn't it because of him? How could I otherwise have known joy over nothing, if I hadn't been given joy? How little joy is enough?

I was often alone at Grandad's farm too, but I was a different kind of alone there. He kept an eye on me. Looked me straight in the eye. Listened. Laughed without making a sound. Sat quietly. There were meals, conversations, good silences. All the sorts of things kids thrive on.

That's right, Grandad would say. *You'll see. It's fine. It'll be fine*, he would say. *No problem. It's really no problem.*

Grandad's presence in intermittent, cautious circles around me was out of respect, not out of fear or uncertainty. Almost with reverence, I've thought to myself since – the way he would come and see I was in bed, pull the duvet over me when I was younger, the way he stood by the door, asked if there was enough light. Should the door be a bit more shut? Was everything okay?

The closest he came to nagging was *Would you like something? Are you hungry, thirsty, some milk, squash? I've got some biscuits in the pantry. Don't you want anything? Are you sure there's nothing you'd like?* So much that we used to laugh about it.

And then he would sit down at his place by the kitchen table with his arms folded in front of him on the table, collapsed, but always upright, and say: *Well that's fine, then.*

And then he would say nothing, maybe for hours.

He could sit staring across the room, out of the window without saying anything – and still seem to be doing something. He would sit quite still at the kitchen table with a cup of coffee listening to the radio. It was the opposite of Mum's posture on the sofa at home – her hands constantly occupied rolling cigarettes and with the ashtray, coffee, crosswords and magazines. A silence that sucked in all sounds and became deafening.

Grandad's silence was just silent, making room for other sounds. His name was Ragnvald. When he died, something flipped over and it was totally up to me.

That was when I started cycling so much.

And I refused to accept it, I think, accept that he was dead. *Gone forever.* I don't think I completely believed he was dead, or wanted to believe it, until after Erling moved in a year later and I told him – told him *Grandad's dead.*

I could ask Grandad about things. And then he would look at me and say *Well, you know what, Margrete,* and then came long speeches. I have a photo of us on the tractor – and how happy we are! Such big smiles. I'm about five or six. It's a late sunny Easter. The earth is black with patches of glassy white snow.

The smell of damp earth. *That's* what I mean.

"Grandad, what's my dad's name?"

He looked straight at me, saying nothing.

He leant over the tractor engine again, removed a part and studied it carefully, blew at it, wiped it, glancing at the yard. He looked at me.

"I think you'd better talk to your mum about *that*."

"She won't tell me."

"No."

He continued to examine the engine part for a while, but his thoughts were focused on our conversation.

"No, we'll just have to wait then."

He sighed slightly, dried his hands on a rag, and looked me straight in the eye.

"Till she wants to talk about it. Let's go in now, Margrete. We could do with a cup of coffee, couldn't we?"

Spring came early. All the snow had gone and the yard was bare. It was blustery and the sun was high, but the wind was stronger. It ripped, it banged. The dirt flew. The farm was exposed, surrounded by the fields and trees coming into leaf, pale green flowing veils. As if the whole world at any time might sweep across the farm.

Later in the day the wind dropped somewhat, and the air was suddenly ice-cold wet in the sun.

"Is he dead?"

It wasn't easy to ask, even though Grandad was easy to talk to. I nattered away at Grandad's, the uninhibited way kids can just talk and talk and talk (something I didn't do again until I was an adult).

I tried to ask casually while Grandad was measuring spoonfuls of coffee into the pot. He stopped with the spoon mid-air and looked at me.

"Margrete ... I don't know. I really don't know. I bet it

snows again," he added, looking outside. He counted the spoonfuls of coffee, and stood there while it brewed.

"How do you know *that*, Grandad?"

"What?"

"That it's going to snow."

"Well, you know …"

"But how? It's so sunny!"

"Well yes, but I can feel it, you see. I can feel it on Stella's nose."

I laughed. Grandad gave a contented smile.

He went and let Stella in. The dog came into the room wagging her tail, and scurried over to her bowl next to the fridge – bringing with her a hint of the icy air outside.

"You're a good girl too," said Grandad, looking affectionately at his old dog.

I drank squash and ate plain Marie biscuits for a while. Grandad slurped his boiling hot coffee.

"Grandad?"

"Yes?"

"Why do you call Stella a girl?"

"Because she's a girl dog, a bitch. But I talk a lot of nonsense, you know, Margrete. Don't listen to everything I say."

He chuckled.

"Grandad, do you know what the banana said to the dog?"

"No ..."

"Nothing – bananas can't talk!"

He smiled, looking straight at me with amusement.

"But Margrete, do you know why the banana went to the doctor's?"

"Because it slipped?"

"No, because it wasn't peeling well."

"Oh …"

"Got you there, didn't I?"

"Tell me about when I was little, Grandad."

"When you were little?"

He went and poured himself another cup and sat down opposite me again.

His body was heavy, but his movements were close and precise.

We had our fixed places. He sat so he could see the yard, and I sat on the bench and could see the fields. There was only daylight in the kitchen. A blue-grey light that made Grandad's eyes even more noticeable.

"Well now. You came into the world one beautiful spring day, you know, and we'd never seen anything like it before. Not around here. What a baby! Goodness me, so sweet! And so white – with big blue eyes. And the day you came home from the hospital, the very same day – you smiled at me. No one would believe me. But it's as true as I'm sitting here. You smiled at me. Looked right at me and smiled. Though you were just a tiny thing. You were born premature, couldn't wait, I'm sure. You slept in with me and Granny, because your mum, she had to stay in hospital for a bit. And when she came and got you, our Stella was so cross she howled all night, so I had to put her outside. And how you tucked into your milk! Drank your bottle like a motherless calf, you did. Looked right at us and sucked. A proper ray of sunshine, you were. Cried when you were hungry, but otherwise as good as gold. Of course Stella wanted you here!"

"How long did I live here?"

"Well, it must have been some … a while."

This is my story of creation. A ray of sunshine. Both with and without a mother.

"Mum, what happened when I was born?"

"What?"

She was sitting on the sofa. I was at the table doing homework. (I could see the whole flat from there, I had an overview of all the rooms. I always did my homework in the sitting room, even though I had a desk in my room.)

"Why did you have to stay in hospital when I was born?"

She was silent. Stiff. Her eyes narrowed.

"Did Grandad tell you that?"

"Mmm."

She took a deep breath (I've no idea when she ever breathed out again).

"There's nothing more to say. It's so long ago."

◊ ◊ ◊

And while I lay awake in my bed after drinking cocoa at Erling's, and it rained, and later, in the following weeks, well into September, while I sat by the window and watched Erling come home from work and leave again – there was this feeling I can't explain, which everything depended on.

I can't explain what it was, but it seemed inseparable from me. Perhaps it was just the feeling of – the world in me? Or me in the world. The interaction between us.

I floated and floated around and around the funfair, the closed market stalls, the raffle ticket stalls, between people and rides, candyfloss and chicken wings.

There were dodgems, huge teacups to sit in that spun around their own axis and round and round on an iron platform that again spun and turned and tipped, so you were slung round in an intermittent suction sensation.

There was a small merry-go-round for children, with different animals to sit on, at a snail's pace.

And then there was a bit bigger one with swings that swung a long way out when the merry-go-round picked up speed, sluggish.

There was centrifugal force and speed in colours and restrictions, and it cost a lot of money.

I floated and floated around the fairground until I knew that an adult would soon spot me and ask if I wasn't too young to be out alone, or call one of the security guards, and I turned to go home.

That was when it happened.

I saw one of the guards coming my way and I sneaked behind one of the stalls, found an open door and slipped inside, so he wouldn't find me.

The night was filled with summer. The air was so bursting with growth that, if it hadn't been for the drought and the almost imperceptible hint of chill at night, the world would have opened and withered like a plant. Maybe with a blossom on each branch ... The air was so open in the summer night that it was shiny black with an almost imperceptible hint of frost, the frost that would come in September, and in the form of rain the day after.

And that's how the world was balanced, just about. The growth was held back.

Afterwards I cycled home with clear, dark air over my face.

The speed made the night air flow like fresh water over my skin. My skin was exposed to the night's piercing touch –

extremely pure and pale beneath the blood. Congealing, sticky blood.

My breath was hard in my throat, heavy in my lungs. I pedalled so fast that my neck was almost contorted by my piercingly quick breath.

And then there's this *something* I know, but still can't explain – which saved me.

For I actually think it wasn't only because of Erling that I survived, when he carried me up to his flat from my refuge under the stairs. Made cocoa. I think I would have survived without him.

I have never lost myself completely.

And later in life too, if I have been disheartened, desperate, there's always something that saves me; I know this, but can't explain it. It always comes back to me. And it might almost seem that the more I knew then – that loneliness is boundless, that loneliness goes on and on in suffocation and impossibility – the more I resisted. The more I knew that Erling would move again, disappear from my life – that it wouldn't last, that he wasn't mine – the stronger I became. The more I knew that it would never end and that I was the boundary, the only boundary …

I sat under the stairs and listened at night, listened intensely and was silently desperate for something I was sure was out there somewhere. Cycled it, silenced it. Frantic. It was Erling. It was also the August night itself, the way I was in it. It was the rain. It was the future I have had, which I knew then would come.

It is an upside down, defiant logic.

Was it raw force? And raw will?

◊ ◊ ◊

At night our block of flats was quiet and dark, even though the light was on in the lobby. I sat looking at the dark stone floor, the brick walls, listening. I had white socks, brownish grey with dirt, and plasters on my knees – I sat there picking off the scab on my knee, and keenly felt the movements of what had happened in my breath.

The late August night was chilled all the way in, yet it gleamed with fire somewhere far inside my life.

And this something, this nothing, drove me on.

I walked home alone from school one day in September, slowly, silently in myself – and there was another kind of light somewhere else too. Constant light? Seen in the leaves. In the growth of late summer. In the overgrown and wilting damp, along the little path from the school car park and the football pitch to our car park and on down to Brinken. Along the path, the colourless stalks gilded by icy frost against suddenly hot, still high, late morning sun.

I nearly disappeared into myself in the hallway, and was about to reveal everything when I looked up and saw Erling standing by his car, then shutting the car door as he turned towards our building.

I ran towards him. My rucksack flapped open. I held the shoulder straps as I trotted along, balancing my rucksack and gym bag.

"Hi!"

"Hi, Margrete!"

And I was back in the world, in Erling's world, where there was room for everything – including me, and my secret.

But to tell it meant being cut open, dying, because the secret was part of me.

Erling had large, summer-brown hands. His skin shone in the

fresh, new rain-filled air. His skin came so close to mine through the air. The deep furrow in his forehead, and on either side of his mouth, how he smelt … always. And I knew that I would make it, the time I walked beside him into our building, I knew I would make it. Because I had to.

Nowadays I gauge my childhood struggles with the awareness of an adult that gladly holds a child's hand, and I recognise my struggles back then as a demand. But I didn't suffer any injuries as a child. Mum was never cruel. And not knowing who my father was didn't bother me, I actually think it helped me. I think the fact that I didn't know who my father was meant I had an essential, open space for pure fantasy that helped me imagine another world. My world. I imagined all sorts of things. I notice that I'm reluctant to call them daydreams – that would diminish the meaning of them and might lead one to doubt the reality of this open space. Any man could be my father, in theory. Erling, for instance; someone like him.

And the same way that people in prison can dream about life outside, I dreamt about becoming an adult.

But remembering how this young Margrete appeared to herself is like taking on an incredible strength that strangely enough is impossibly hard to know about now.

The lip gloss I stole at the shopping centre in Kløfta, I remember that, that's easy to remember. I stood there, no big deal, as though I had done nothing but steal things my whole life, I stood there looking at a basket of eyeshadows on a table just inside the door of the perfume shop. A door that opened directly onto the shopping centre's walkway. I concentrated intensely, caught the shop assistant's eye, heavy with baby-blue eyeshadow, and smiled at her. The smile was mine, completely real. Without blinking. And she looked down again at something she was pricing, and I took the lip gloss in my hand and slowly walked out. Not fast, not too slowly. I just took it and left.

Imagine mastering the border between me and the world like that. I never did it again. The lip gloss represented this insight, and my destiny. The scent of abstracted orange in a small glass cylinder …

I also know about these absolute conditions of an open-abstract approach that we inhabited as children – empty, open forms that were the basis of play, and life. It was an approach, unprepared but searched for and aimed at a particular condition, a way of being.

When we heard that Åsa in our class was dead, when we were in class 6, I know that we were sitting in the classroom on the corner with a view of the music school and the road home to the flats. I shared a table with Kamilla and Johanne and Marianne. They cried. I felt I was frozen in a game where I couldn't move, and I longed to get out, desperately. Had to get under the stairs, into my bed, sit by the window in my room.

And it wasn't just that my crying, being non-existent, was taboo. It was much more.

I sat staring out of the window at the small wood of birch trees between the school and the flats. There was a faint breeze in the tall, pale green silver birches. And then there was this cobalt-blue evening glow in me. The pale green summer night. A black light. Grey-white mornings under the stairs. A form of wonder.

◊ ◊ ◊

"Are *you* going to go to the Jessheim Festival?"

I met Kamilla by the playground at school. She had just come back from a holiday abroad. She was happy and full of energy. And all her foreignness, what it means to travel abroad, was as clear to me as my longing for her foreign travel and its self-evidence.

First we played French skipping for a while, then we ran down to the parallel bars on the edge of the football pitch.

Kamilla was going to the Jessheim Festival in the evening with her parents and big sister and she wanted me to go with them. And I just knew I couldn't.

I didn't have any money and saying that I couldn't afford it would involve so much more, which I thought should have been obvious to them and which I still couldn't reveal. I didn't want to go with them anyway. There was something about the thought of being with them that day that was oppressive, decisive in a way, and it seemed impossible to get involved in that kind of decision.

"I don't know," I said.

"Oh come on," she said. "It'll be fun."

Some of the older boys arrived on their bikes to play football. Kamilla and I sat on one of the bars and watched them. We talked about nothing, just had a conversation. We talked about us.

We talked about everything.

We talked about who was the best looking of the boys playing football. I chose Aslak. Kamilla chose Christoffer.

I wish I had wanted to go the Jessheim Festival. I felt drawn by the unspoken, all-embracing joy of having real friends. Soulmates. (This was before I met Erling – I knew of him, but I didn't yet know anything for certain, or his name)

"I don't know if I can," I said when Kamilla asked again.

I had worn my favourite red T-shirt, the one I got for my birthday in May. A denim skirt. I pulled off my clothes, cut them into bits, as if I was programmed to do so, and put them in a rubbish bag with the coffee grounds that were still in the pot – a plastic bag that I tied tightly and put in yet another bag that I tied tightly and threw down the rubbish chute, while I thought about what I would say to Mum if she unexpectedly asked about the T-shirt and the skirt.

I wore my hair in a ponytail. It reached down to the middle of my back, a reassuring and wavering weight against my body.

We swung on the bars. I hung by my arms and knees sweeping the ground with my ponytail. Back and forth, back and forth. We swung around and around the iron bar until our hips got faint purple bruises. Swish, again, swish, around and around, and again. And my ponytail beat lightly on the ground each time.

It was as if the heat was turning in on itself. It was as if it had to happen, it had been so hot the whole summer, without rain, and something had to happen.

The heat was so dry and pervasive that it took over everything – the heat encompassed everything until there was nothing but dry heat. But then the light from the heat was so sharp, too, that all things were glaringly distinct.

I wore clogs without socks. They were so used that the wooden soles felt like soft leather. They had been red once, but were now so worn that they were greyish. They lay one here and one there in the dry grass while we sat barefoot on the bars, blue-painted iron, scratched and rusty, watching the big boys play football.

Kamilla changed her mind, she wanted Aslak too. But he was mine. He was mine because I saw him how I saw him. And because I had said it first.

Then Kamilla had to go home. We went back to the school, where we had left our bikes. The dust on the tarmac was almost hovering in the dry air. There was dust everywhere. In my skirt pocket, where I kept my skipping elastic and lip gloss, there were small grains of dirt. In the lid of the lip gloss there were tiny grains of dirt in the sticky goo that had leaked out and been screwed in.

"Oh please come! We're going after supper. Just come with us – it's no problem," said Kamilla.

"I've got to ask Mum first."

"Okay."

"I'll come if I'm allowed."

I was happy, hopeful.

And I really was happy and hopeful as I stood there talking to Kamilla in the heat, as I said *Bye* and she answered *Bye then* and cycled up to Jessheim while I cycled down to the flats.

Kamilla was nice. I liked her. We sat at the same desk at school, next to each other, helping each other (we talked, swapping ideas and right answers). And now I wish I had wanted to go with Kamilla and her family to the Jessheim Festival. It didn't feel like a lie. It wasn't false. I wanted to ask Mum and go with them. There was something else that was wrong – that I didn't really want to go with them, and couldn't say it how it was. That was what was wrong.

I often said I had to ask Mum about things, but never did, and told myself that it wasn't lying; it wasn't a big lie, at least, it was open, and openly directed at me. In a way it was to help out, to help Mum, to give the truth a face, as she didn't have the strength to say yes or no and make up her mind about the Jessheim Festival. But I knew that she thought about it. Or rather, I knew that I wished she would think about that sort of thing. And when I saw her staring into space, and once in a while when our eyes met, then I saw that she wished she could make up her mind, that she wanted me to keep away from anything that could be dangerous. She wanted me to be home at a reasonable time, and fall asleep in my bed. She wanted everything to be full up and welcoming and fine. That was really what she said. Those evasive looks in her eyes, they meant that I asked her and she answered yes or no.

Because it's not that truth doesn't have words, that there aren't words for it. I have never had the feeling many have spoken about, the feeling that it's not possible to say things, that there aren't words for things. I have always understood that words are endless and that it's possible to say not just anything, but also to tell the precise truth.

I can in one simple sentence say what happened at the Jessheim Festival, but I don't know what it would mean for others; I mean, I don't know if people would agree on what it involves, what the words mean. (And I want to decide, I want to help decide what it means, how it can be understood.)

◊ ◊ ◊

Before Mum went to work that evening, I was troubled – and sure. But I hadn't yet made a decision. I wished I had wanted to go. I decided to go several times, went down all the stairs, sat on the bottom step, waiting for someone to come, as if they would be bound to see what I was fretting about, and as if it was extremely important to keep it hidden – and then I went up again.

It happened again.

It was as if there was a demand somewhere. Something was left undone, unaccounted for.

Something needed a decision, a correction.

I could have easily used my food money and maybe defrosted some supper, I thought, or I could have said that something cost more than it did. But I couldn't do that either.

I watched children's TV. It was *Summer on Mirabell Island*, a paradise, as I remember it – a paradise in pure colours from summer holidays by the sea that I could only dream about, but were mine, I felt; they were just as much mine even though I could only dream about them. The dreams were just as much mine as the reality of Mirabell Island was for others, maybe more so.

I sat in my room for a while, by the window. I could hear the fairground up in Jessheim. I heard Mum make coffee and sit down on the sofa. I saw her through the walls. I sensed her movements in my nerves. Her sighs were sighs within me. Deep inside my stomach. But I couldn't sigh her sighs. I had to keep them suspended in the air, untouched, like a juggler; I could never let them fall into the silence of my stomach. And to keep her sighs suspended, I had to grab them before they fell, I had to feel the precise weight of her sighs to know how much strength I should use when I threw them up, and to know when they would fall. I knew how Mum sighed, how her body stiffened on the sofa – she collapsed into herself while her fingers automatically reached for her pouch of tobacco, Petterøe's 3, tapped out some tobacco, took the paper between two fingers, so precisely, while she glanced up, suddenly (almost like an animal), up at the hall, *Margrete, are you there?* And then she would look down again while she arranged the tobacco, rolled it expertly, slightly moistened the paper while my *Yes* resounded through the hall and into her. Then she lit the cigarette, breathed out and leant back.

I joined her to watch the news.

"I'm going to go out for a bit," I said afterwards.

And when she went to work, I was sitting at the bottom of the stairs.

"Bye."

"Bye then."

It had got so late that I was sure Kamilla and her family would have left – and I set off on my bike.

I often went out at night after Mum had gone to work, not so much out of restlessness as in a systematic-automatic quest, like a job, out of necessity, through the dusk, and after dark, especially in the summer. On my bike.

I could now hear the music playing up in Jessheim, all the way down to the flats.

The music, or the fact that the music reached all the way down to us, inside the flat, made the flat even emptier. It sucked the dim-lit rooms out of themselves, and shut the darkness in. Turning the lights on made no difference, it only emphasised how the space was sucked out.

The evening air was refreshingly sunless.

I always pedalled fast. Very fast. This time I raced up there, left my bike in the ditch down by the town hall and waited until the guards had gone across to the other side. Then I climbed over the high fence that had been put up around the fairground area.

This was all part of the same steady flow as the bike ride, fast and invisible. And I got over without being spotted.

I stood on the inside of a door I had never seen, never gone through. But I had always been there.

I stood looking in at a darkness that opened itself back inside me. I think Mum was there somewhere in the dark. And I was in there with her. I had always been there. And I knew all about her in there. But she was silent, so was I. I could just run down the stairs, get on my bike, race off.

But there was a limit to how far I could go on my bike.

I often cycled as far as the library – over the motorway, past the Jessheim crossroads and along to the old, white wooden building by Nordby school, Jessheim library. It smelt of old, dirty wood and greasy book dust. The old librarian wore a brown lab coat and had piercing eyes. I borrowed all the books by Victoria Holt, almost feeling I had stolen something.

Lots of times I went further, right up to Nordby lake. And once I cycled even further, on past the college, and past Svenskestusletta, until there was nothing but forest on both sides. The soil at the edge of the road was heavy with silence. Dark stretches of fir trees furrowed further and further in towards an endless blackness.

I knew that Sweden was on the other side of the forest east of Jessheim. I knew that the Earth was round, that you could go all the way round. I knew it was possible to emigrate, to America, for instance. Even so, there was also a place that was just further into the woods, that went on and on in a forest of fir trees. In America too. In the big ships that drifted steadily over the Atlantic Ocean to America, too. A bigger ocean than I could imagine – *that* big.

And I knew there were open hillsides of raspberry bushes in areas of cleared woodland, and paths upon paths further and further in. Grandad and I used to go for walks in the forest. And Grandad's deep insight into the forest was also a part of it.

Every autumn we went on long walks to pick berries –
heavy, sweaty warmth in wellies when it was neither autumn
nor summer. Cold when we cycled there in the morning, hot
while we picked raspberries on an open hillside, where we sat
and had our packed lunch. Wasps with their buzzing stings of
silence and concentrated late-summer sun. The odd word now
and then, maybe just *Oh, look at this big one,* or other things,
more important, and it was recorded in the world like a
thought, but between us. Measuring who had picked the
most...

In the Easter holidays Grandad made ski tracks for me in the
field. We sat against the barn wall, our eyes closed in the sharp
new sun as if we were in the mountains. We had a knapsack
and ski wax, tartan thermoses, one with coffee and one with
cocoa, oranges and milk chocolate.

Grandad was buried in the cemetery in Hovin. We never went
there, but after Erling moved away from Jessheim, I cycled over
and planted wood anemones on Grandad's grave.

The cars on the motorway, single cars, sometimes two at once,
roared past me in the open split of a road between the fir trees,
as I cycled further and further north.

I wasn't afraid. Or was fear and solitude necessary for me?
Did I need to be in this borderland of fear and solitude not to be
sliced in two – so that the part of me where the incident was
preserved wouldn't be cut out, and me with it? I had to enter
the solitude to always manage to be one step ahead of it. I had
to cycle through it and let it sink in. Let the incident sink into
my muscles, into an ocean. Cross an ocean ...

My fear of the flat was also a fear I knew I would one day
have to confront, and overcome – *I must, I will* – and it's like I

pedalled even more frantically, spent even more time outside, to prepare myself. It was a preparatory gesture, an absorption of the flat's foundations. To one day be able to take a bunch of wood anemones home and give it to Mum again, although she might get tears in her eyes and turn away …

She hadn't turned away to conceal her emotions, that time I ceremoniously presented her with a bunch of wood anemones, like other mothers might have done. She had turned away to conceal the fact that there was *too* great a distance between my bitter-fresh joy, my insistently bright eyes, and her helplessness.

But I never got off my bike in dense forest. I pedalled fast so no one would see me. I was such speed. And I went so far. Several times I cycled all the way to Kløfta. (How long would this have taken me? It's almost five miles!)

I got off my bike when I reached the fields outside Kløfta, I sat at the edge of the road, the edge of the field, just intending to sit there and watch the cars go past. I sat hidden at the roadside, almost consumed by it.

There were leaden skies over the fields of barley in June, dark mint. The fresh, wet summer chill pierced warm muscles, warm skin. And the shiny black rain didn't start until I was back at the flats in the early evening. An early summer evening when the world was being hemmed in by foliage and branches in strong, wet wind, just as I cycled so precisely up to the white brick wall, and leant my bike against it (because the kickstand was broken). And I ran up the stairs, with the thick mercury rain pounding coldly against the roof hatch at the top of the stairway, above my head. My red wool jumper was full of grass stains and the smell of rain.

I got in just before Mum left. Said *Bye*. I ran back down again and sat under the stairs.

I sat there under the sound of the rain, under the fading lead light, until it was black. I went on waiting without waiting. I waited for something without knowing what it was. The way I sat at the side of the road noting down the colour and speed of cars. Counting cars. Writing makes of cars and registration numbers in a small yellow notebook. Spring. Summer. Autumn. Made a note when the train came from town. The express train to the south sliced through the fields. Slicing the future, building bridges that couldn't be burnt, but which disappeared into thin air and lay ready again in the same swoosh.

I had an awful dream at that time. I think it was only once, a one-off dream. I blame it on Idi Amin. It was about African children, mashed African children, masses of African children that flooded the road down by Brinken, at the crossroads near where Johanne lived. Just before the turning down to Johanne's in my class, there was a dip in the road that in the spring became a small, brown lake. Wasn't there a drain at the bottom of it that got blocked? Like in an inverted well, I was sucked down inside, inside a well that overflowed with an incinerated mess of bleeding, mashed African children, brown, like poo, with blood: an outhouse, like the sewage-filled stream in the woods on the other side of Brinken. But the well was shallow, shallow like puddles, like the pools of water where we made dams and played in the spring. The well was from the depth of the surface. The drain was blocked, oozing with blood and crushed children. Oozing and oozing. The nightmare was shameful. I couldn't think about it.

When this nightmare appeared in my mind, I had to shut it in, and whenever Uganda has been mentioned in some context or other since then, I have had a feeling that there has been something I have known about the consequences beyond what can be measured. It's only now that I remember what it is.

I watched TV a lot. Watched the news. It was safe. They continued talking whatever happened, every single day, every evening. And they smiled at the end. Wasn't TV friendlier in those days, actually? Educational and helpful? Adults who didn't play at being children or teenagers but played at being adults, conversing about things other than the obvious. I watched tennis from Wimbledon, got drawn into the game, was there myself, with the spectators, I was there in the arms of the players, again and again. I watched *The Onedin Line* and *Edward VII*. That music! If it hadn't been for the TV and radio, I wouldn't have been given that music, and I wonder what kind of life *that* would have been …

I always pushed the armchair right up against the wall when I watched TV. Then I could see the whole sitting room, the hall door and the balcony door. With nothing behind me.

And then there was that rush of utter emptiness when the last programme was over … It was a flat, oppressive feeling, without lamplight. Like the nights when Erling was away. It was as if there had been a power cut and I didn't have any fuses. The power was off outside too, the streetlights, everywhere, and nothing could be done about it. Like a spring night in late April, for instance – *that* cold greyness. No insulating snow and burning cold. No temperate steam-heat off the ground on a sunny day. But a flat, insisting cold that crept into your bone marrow and didn't leave.

It was before they asphalted the roads around Brinken, and it smelt of earth and water and the ground felt soft underfoot when you walked.

That first day of wearing shoes again after a winter with boots! Always the first days of wearing shoes – the thrill you have room for as a child, and which takes on the smell of spring forever.

In the spring the road down to Brinken was paradise, with shifting amounts of sludge, small and large puddles, strong currents, small streams.

We dug ditches and built dams and conquered each other's countries and played skipping games. And I had a social advantage in the spring – I was good at French skipping. I was a popular French skipping partner. We could play for hours down at Brinken car park. The ground there was perfectly soft and firm. It was best when it had been raining and the dirt had nearly, only nearly, dried again – like a springboard.

We had our own world of orderly movements and dripping muscular ecstasy reaching deep inside us. There were two on each team and it was an advantage to be tall and supple when the elastic rose above thighs, waists, under the arms, neck, then was held up high.

Just knowing that Erling was there, in our block of flats.

Knowing that he would leave again too, that he wasn't mine. He was an adult, I was a child. And I knew I had to make this one destiny, this imperative – Erling – into something inside me, if I were to survive the fact he wasn't mine.

I sat by my window and it rained in the spring; I sat by the half-open window with grey holes of rain clouds surging upwards and sideways – and I got this clear view of everything, reflected back on me.

I was shut in a room with doors I could unlock just by being there, just by snapping my fingers – and then the loneliness and emptiness became even worse, when I breathed it away.

It was the rooms themselves I couldn't get rid of. I *was* those rooms, but I couldn't be them, I had to vomit them out, breathe them out, as light as air. But Mum was there and I had to carry the rooms with me like big fields in my hands, in the spokes of my bike, in every millimetre of breath.

I cycled all the way to Kløfta, sat down in the shade outside the shopping centre and just sat there. Sat outside Kløfta shopping centre, by the entrance to the car park at the back. A flat, simple tarmac ocean of mobility, easy to follow. That's where I sat. I knew no one there. And no one knew me.

I would sing along to "Kathy's Song" in those days, without knowing what I was singing. Something about being like the rain, standing alone …

Today I cry playing Simon and Garfunkel's cassette over and over. Now I understand it, what it means, and I knew it at the time. I never cried then. Now I cry. There were sounds of words I didn't understand, but which meant what the music meant, and what I felt, what I wanted to think … about what happened, about Erling, how he changed everything.

Crying now seems to be the link between my silent knowledge at the time and broader silent knowledge now. The truth of the only truth I knew.

I must have cycled many, many miles a week when I was young. Cycling standing up! Pedalling at such a speed down from the motorway towards Brinken that I stood up tall and was the wind, but broke through the wind too, exceptionally clear, a dash in the world. Through the world. Controlled, neck-breaking speed. An extreme joy. Warm skin from chilly spring wind. Clear yet invisible.

And the white-blue winter light at midday.

Going home from school in the winter, between the snowbanks, with the stiff cold tearing at my face.

The blue afternoons when I knew that Mum was on the sofa, awake, and I *had to* go home ...

The huge piles of snow in the car park down by Brinken, near where Johanne lived. The snow holes we made, the hours we spent on them. I was outside after my early supper until late at night. We made snow holes with tunnels between them. We never finished them, because when we had finished one hole, we soon started planning new directions, digging new tunnels and creating more marvels in the snow.

Making such thin snow hole walls that the hole was filled with blue-lit ice skin. Walls made of diamonds. Sitting in snow for hours. Sinking into the smell of glass-blue, coarse-crystal snow.

King of the castle. Nosebleeds in snow – a knot in the chest, a weight in the stomach.

Olav from the other block of flats had picked a fight with me and I pushed him, right onto Johanne's boots, which were on their way up and met Olav's face on the way down ... He really hurt himself and was furious, hit me on the nose so it bled. He wanted revenge for the time we had had a proper fight. *Chicken, chicken*, we called after him, as I wiped the blood off with a lump of snow.

I'd once had a serious fight with Olav. He was in my class. We fought down by the football pitch in Døli. At the primary school. It was before what happened at the Jessheim Festival. I was maybe ten or eleven. He had ruined the house that Lina and I had made in the small wood of birch trees behind our playground. He had discovered our secret house and taken it over with his friends, and they had ruined it. It was unforgivable. We didn't like him anyway. He used to follow us around. Didn't leave us alone. He had to be taught a lesson. It was all a game I played. And I was the angriest about being harassed. And the fastest.

Lina and her brothers stood around us shouting *We want blood, we want blood. Come on, Margrete, get him, knock him down, headbutt him in the gut.* And I hit him hard. I noticed how good I was at fighting. I dodged his blows. Intensely focused.

The others cheered me on even more. *Come on, come on.*

Then I was suddenly interrupted, in the middle of the fight, by myself. I felt how I was both the blows and the person behind the blows and it gave me a power kick, that it was me … but this interrupted force had nothing to do with Olav, what he had done, the house, the game, the pestering, Lina and the others. It was horrible to have him there, inside me, where there was such a force inside me, where I was so near what was me…

I stopped fighting. Started running towards the flats, turned round and shouted:

"I can't be bothered with this, it's stupid. You're just stupid. You're all stupid."

For Olav this meant he'd lost – that's what it's like when you fight with girls. Girls aren't supposed to fight, so it was fine with me; I didn't lose face, it was fine that I gave in, because that's what girls are like. And I won, double.

◊ ◊ ◊

In the winter, when I came in and Mum was home, the flat was dark. She would often be half-asleep on the sofa. Perhaps it was her day off. Then everything was uncertain, a long quivering disquiet. Then I left everything be. If she wasn't there, I turned on the lights in the sitting room and my bedroom and the hall.

I always sat on the edge of my bed to pull off my wet clinging tights, which had stuck to my damp ice-cold thighs. I hung them to dry in the bathroom. Left my sodden mittens on the stove in the sitting room. Made cocoa. Put the light on, and the TV. Fried myself an egg, maybe. Filled the flat with a faint frying smell and yellow lamplight. And there was a kind of purity in the winter, a purity of silence, that eased the longing. The winter blacked out one place and lit up another.

I perhaps remember best what it means to keep quiet, to never be the one to ruin the atmosphere, add to Mum's burden, ruin what is always possible.

To keep well away. Away from all games, all people. To be clear in myself.

I used to wander around after the others had gone in. I lived by the high banks of snow. Knew so well the nuances from afternoon to evening and deeper, even deeper night. The lights in people's houses were extra clear from the blue-black intervals between the streetlights, where I walked close to the edge of the snow.

One time when Mum hadn't come home by the morning, I pretended nothing had happened. And after dark that day, when she had come home and gone to sleep, I went down and rang the bell at Johanne's house to ask if Johanne could come out and play.

Mum was home – and the flat was even emptier, filled with her sleep and disquiet.

There wasn't any snow. The road was bare and frozen brown, hard. The puddles were glazed, crunching under me as I went down to Brinken, to Johanne's.

I crushed every puddle's brittle ice on the way down.

It was almost night-dark, after children's TV. An autumn evening before the snow arrived. And in the kitchen window at Johanne's there shone a small yellowish light.

It was as if the dark of evening was reversed against a bigger light further inside their house. A mysterious place that was neither the rooms, nor the house, nor the people in it. Johanne's family. Her sisters, Anna and Sigrid. Her mum and dad. It was a place they seemed to own quite naturally, or rather, it was almost impossible to separate them from it. But this magical quality was something other than them, other than their house; it was quite obviously something outside of them, and something they owned. It was therefore possible to acquire.

Johanne's mother opened the door.

"Hello, Margrete!"

It smelt of buns, green soap and, faintly, of old rose perfume. (Johanne's mother's perfume was always out in the bathroom. With those antique yellow walls and that soft-brass lighting.)

"Is Johanne there?"

I stood outside on their steps, just where the indoor light met the autumn evening.

"Yes. Hold on a minute."

Johanne appeared and said *Hi*.

"Hi, are you coming out then?"

"I can't. We're having people round soon and …"

And then her mother came and said that anyway it was too late to go out now.

"But you can come and play with Johanne inside for a bit. How about that?"

I said something about forgetting how late it was and that I really had to go home now anyway.

"Hold on, Margrete," said Johanne's mum. "I'll get you a bun to eat on the way."

And I walked back with a bun in each hand and a heaviness in my chest because Johanne's mother had seen right into our flat where Mum lay sleeping, where Mum hadn't come home from work, and seen what it meant.

The buns were white like a cartoon with Christmas music, white like new snow. Chalky white buns with icing sugar. There wasn't a single brown spot on the buns and they melted in my mouth like big, buttery chocolates. One bun in each hand – hands without mittens, icy cold.

And I walked back to the flats, at home outside between the streetlights and the crunchy crushed puddles.

There were other times, too, when Mum hadn't come home from work, and hadn't told me that I needed to be on my own even longer.

She had probably just forgotten, I thought to myself. I sat up in bed, waiting for her to come, and the whole building shrunk into my bed while the world outside loomed huge.

I wouldn't have said I was scared at the time. I would have said that I was maybe a bit worried about her. I would have said that I was used to being home alone. That I knew she would come, I knew *that*, and I didn't mind …

But I was so fundamentally and terribly scared that my fear encompassed everything and made it essential to create a space around me – a fearless space.

I sat up in bed until I heard her come in. I sat there thinking that I was Margrete in a different flat – in a fantasy story about Johanne's house with voices and lights that went on and on, as though the house was endless inside. Walls receding into the distance with voices and conversations around tables that kept going without me having to pay attention. A place where I could let all my strength follow the adult voices talking and telling me more than on TV even, more than teachers at school, like in the books I knew existed – and I was that story.

When I heard Mum come in, something let go in my chest, and took another kind of hold. A gnawing relief, possible hardness, a lot more, which I let sink all the way in … and which I snuggled down with under my duvet.

I lay there listening until I heard she had gone to bed. And I almost fainted with exhaustion.

Falling asleep like fainting – a stiff body that crumples into a softness outside of everything, becoming heavy with open dreams. The fearless space crushed and surrendered to the night again. Ready to be scared again, next time.

It's probably impossible to survive without dreams. This was before Erling moved into the flat across the hallway. Before what happened at the Jessheim Festival. If he had been living there then, I would have gone over and got a good night's sleep.

◊ ◊ ◊

So I went to school the day after I was supposedly sick. I wrote a note saying *I wasn't at school yesterday, 18 August 1975, because I had an upset stomach. Margrete.* And I said that *Mum was asleep, you see*, when the teacher asked why Mum hadn't signed it.

Everyone kept talking about what had happened.

We stood outside school before we went home, talking about

what had happened.

"He was still alive when they found him, you know. Can you believe it? He was just lying there, bleeding to death."

"Shit!"

"Unbelievable. Bleeding to death."

"It was Ronny and his mates that did it."

"How do you know?"

"*Everybody* knows."

Kamilla had got a new hairband at the Jessheim Festival, made of velvet or something. She had a leather rucksack, the kind you instinctively knew was the right kind of rucksack. In the little zipped pocket on the front, she kept her red raspberry lip gloss. It wasn't completely cylindrical, it was wider round the top. The glass was yellowish. It had a red screw cap and there was a red plastic flowery pattern on the glass, so the surface wasn't smooth.

I stood opposite her outside school, I had a stomach ache and wanted to go home, away from them. And I had a definite feeling that even if the lip gloss I had pinched was much cheaper and unlike the lip gloss any of the others had (and also stolen merchandise) – it had higher aspirations style-wise.

It was a straight, smooth cylinder of pure glass (after I had removed the label). It had a small, white screw cap and clear orange lip gloss inside. It smelt synthetically sweet and exotically urban. It tasted greasy and grainy. It lived in the orange cat pencil case in my rucksack. A lip gloss that defined my independence, making my loneliness official, pure, orange and real.

My school rucksack was red, thick cotton with white plastic edges that were cracked and worn in the corners. It had a zipped pocket on the flap, where I kept my notebook for messages to our teacher. My rucksack had two straps which I never did up and which knocked against the flap when I ran. It wasn't at all fancy, I knew that, but it was mine, and that made a difference.

While they all walked off towards Jessheim, talking excitedly about what had happened, some silent with terror, others powerfully knowledgeable, I walked slowly, slowly down towards the flats.

I was so scared that I wasn't scared. The fear was me. It was me. And I went stiffly home from school, sinking into the fear. Into their voices, their reality. But then I started running, sucking in earth and water at speed; I heard a car, thought maybe it was Erling, and I breathed deeply, right through the fear, and ran as fast as I could down to the car park by the flats. And it wasn't me. It was so long ago that it wasn't me.

◊ ◊ ◊

It went incredibly fast. When I think about it now, it's as if it had already happened while I sat on the stairs waiting, before I cycled over there that evening. It's as if it happened while I was cycling, while I was floating round and round … Because the incident itself doesn't really exist, it happened so fast, a few minutes, I think, and it was all over, and could never end.

First I sat at the bottom of the stairs, waiting without waiting for anything in particular. And still there was this demand somewhere, this undone thing compelling me.

I still hadn't made a decision, I had, then I hadn't. The sun had gone, it was just beginning to get dark, it was almost clear.

And when the door slammed shut behind Mum, I just knew I had to go. The sound of her car quickly disappeared; it smelt of blue night, music drifting from Jessheim …

My world taken over by light and music, by unknown acquaintances, by my light and my music … clearly, and delicately. There was a tension.

And something had to happen.

Like a fight?

I just wanted to see, to float around invisibly. The music and the fairground were already where I always was. And I just wanted to be there, cycling around as I usually did in the afternoons and evenings.

Johanne lay in bed that night and could hear the music from Jessheim, she lay feeling it right through her, and knew what it was. The night-blue shimmer of pierced love, perhaps, and twisted disappearance, possibly. August night, when August is already a stiff-frozen winter evening. A sharp spring night. Soft summer nights. Midsummer-heavy swimming strokes of darkening cold – leading to relief or a cut. Greedy yellow autumn.

"I don't think I needed to go up there to know," Johanne said when we met again as adults. "I could hear the music, feel the thudding music and night, right inside me. The top window was always open in the summer. The music was nearly cold …"

And I knew too. Before I left, I knew what could happen, what it was. The force of navy blue night. Explosions of blacked out breath.

But I had to go. To find out? To keep an eye on everything?

And the empty flat had no peace, no movement. In the empty flat there was nothing, something worse than nothing.

And what were the odds of something like that happening?

In the warm lamplight of the house where Johanne fell asleep to the sound of drums from Jessheim in the distance, she could be in the darkness completely. She could stare into the light's eyes until the drums left the room erased, without destroying it. To a rhythm she grasped. She could stare into the darkness, stare into the lights until they disappeared in blackness – and still be in them.

On the other side there was an island of light – darker than the dark, lighter than light.

I sat on the bottom step, peeping through my fingers. My bike was leaning against the wall, ready. I cycled over there. The tarmac was thick and rough, hard, but light leaked from down below up into my hands. My grip on the handlebars was firm and easy. Speed spread up through my arms, to my throat and out to my face.

And that's how I always cycled, cycled while I sat still and watched, cycled while I was inside, inside at home, inside at school, inside at other people's houses, alone – that's how I survived – in the realities of dreams, in speed, in light. Is it the shape of me?

◊ ◊ ◊

The circus came in September the year after.

We were really too old for the circus, but Kamilla and I made a thing of it. We loved acrobatics. Kamilla did gymnastics in Kløfta. (I would have too, if I had been able to.)

The circus was in a field by Sand, not far from Grandad's farm. I had read about "The Flying Wappener Brothers", outstanding trapeze artists. And about Rietta Wallenda-Guzman, a 13-year-old tightrope walker who had lost her father, two uncles and an aunt – on a tightrope without a safety net.

And I knew what was special about it long before the circus came, but I didn't know again when it left, and that's why I sat at the roadside waiting.

I sank more and more. Sat outside waiting – and deep inside the banality of everyday existence a black orchid was being carefully digested.

It was a double-edged peace. Not a prayer.

It was more like truth than prayer.

It feels as if that autumn lasts forever, fixed in a fiction that is always also the complete opposite in me – that reveals a reality and makes a fiction real, until at any given time it is autumn, every time it is autumn again, as if for the first time.

And what had happened existed only in me and couldn't, mustn't, be real again for anyone else but me. Yet for me it had to be real or I would disappear in it. And I sat at the roadside writing something shapeless into me. Out to the air. To nothing. The structure of soundlessness. The soundlessness in all sounds.

I sat there, devouring my anxiety. Triple somersaults perfectly executed in my room, the open sky – I knew my slashing movements could deflect the light like a blade.

I was sane at the time of the crime – I knew *that* over and over again.

I had to own what happened. No one else. Just me. There was a law.

"Erling? Hi. What are you up to?"

His door was always open. I went straight in and stood in the middle of his sitting room, as if I had just been passing.

"I'm working," he smiled.

"What kind of work?"

"It's a murder case."

He didn't hesitate, just stared quizzically at me. Carefully.

"Who's been killed?"

"A woman."

I waited, wanting him to say more, wanting to be there. He leant back in his chair, he breathed in, he knew.

"Sit down for a bit, Margrete. Would you like some squash?"

He got up and went into the kitchen. I saw him pour water into the coffee machine, count the spoonfuls of coffee. Then he made me a glass of squash and put it down in front of me.

"Here you are, Margrete," he said.

"Who did it?" I asked eagerly, before he had time to sit down again.

"We know who did it. It was someone she knew, someone she'd been living with. We can prove it was him. But he hasn't confessed. He'll be put on trial. And then there's the sentencing and that sort of thing. The prosecution are going for voluntary manslaughter, we think there are several things that indicate that, and then we need evidence and … We'll see."

"Murdered, wow. But how?"

"She was murdered, yes. We call it manslaughter, but there are different types of manslaughter depending on how it happened … sometimes people are killed by accident, you know."

I sat there with my mouth open. He studied me from more angles than I knew about, but which I sensed, felt.

"What does voluntary manslaughter mean?" I asked, my eyes boring into his face, his arms with rolled up sleeves, grey, faded flannel shirt, thick veins visible under his skin. Strong breath.

He smoothed the hair away from his forehead. He avoided the question and glanced out of the window, down towards Brinken, towards the thick, tall wall of old fir trees in the west. A faint smile spread from the corners of his mouth, from the wrinkles and rooms of unknown strength inside him, which I knew without knowing them. His eyes softened.

"It means ... on purpose," he said.

And it was as though we were talking about something else too. Something other than his job, something other than my secret.

He sat back in his chair at the coffee table, which he used as his desk (and as his kitchen table, as the kitchens in our flats were so small). He had a folder of papers in front of him. He never minded being interrupted. It wasn't possible to interrupt Erling, not like how Mum could be interrupted just rolling a cigarette. She could be irritated if I was just there in the wrong sort of way. I should really have been outside, but inside, at the same time.

"What's the opposite called then, when it's an accident?" I asked, rigid with concentration, as though I had started working on something.

It was raining. Erling had a window open. It smelt of rain in his sitting room. It smelt of cold rain. It smelt of the circus. And a place where I always cried. A tent was always filled with an ice-cold tear, keeping something dry ...

The sawdust reeked of rotting apples and fermentation, of wine and bright lights, with a sharp edge of holy wrath. And then this indescribable *nothing* I lived on, and which the circus performed so brutally and brilliantly.

I cycled over and watched them put up the big top. Went back when they had gone. The force of the black earth, the hard-trodden surface – where the circus had been. When the circus had gone. And the performers were from many countries, they spoke differently, gesticulated differently. They had a freedom.

And after it was all over, they turned their energy towards spring and summer, warming up to all kinds of weather in a day's work and power in hands that grasp other hands in free fall – so many combinations and trapdoors, such big secrets and high lifts, that they keep their mouths soft and warm. Carrying forth the departure and the freedom.

There was a kiss. A constantly acute delight.

I sat there on a hard, ice-cold bench and felt it in my chest. Next to Kamilla. On her right. She was sucking a yellow lollipop. She didn't exist. None of the others existed, at the same time as they formed an endless, complex wall that made the circus's movements extra clear and clearly necessary.

The performers threw dice of light across the ground, dice of music all the way home to the flats.

A victory in each throw. The ground wet with carefully placed warmth. A rough precision.

And the cards are played, the light is gambled away forever, and there's nothing else to demand but victory – an obvious right to backbone and competence in all the darkness.

I was engrossed.

I don't remember Kamilla being there. Don't remember me being there until I reminisce – remember the circus, the weather.

I was the circus, the weather.

I sat staring at the performers, waves of damp, icy wind consuming me. I had music in my blood, music for a pulse. I sat with full concentration, a catcher of light listening for my own listening force to come back to me.

I enjoyed school at the time, and there's a certain similarity, I see now, between the circus and school. There was this very slight, yet fundamental, similarity between the circus and my teacher's voice when she stood still, without gesticulating, without flirting, and told us about historical events that had the force of the circus. And also – it was the circus's and teacher's privilege to give more or less glittering control to this force, or at least an excellent fight.

It rained non-stop that autumn when the circus came.

I cycled over there the day before and watched them put up the big top, cycled back the day after and watched them leave. And they put up the tent in patient expectation of the little girl that I was – the little girl with the memory of raging, red mouth inside her. With grey-flecked eyes. At the end of September. And it was far to cycle – steep hills, long stretches of road.

First I cycled up to the motorway, and disappeared into the big silver birches nearby – hanging gardens of green wind, wet mouth. Raced along under the old maple trees outside Dr Rød's. I cycled down Gardermoveien, reaching an incredible speed. I stood up on the pedals, sucking in relief at the blue landscape that opened onto fields and the Romerike mountain ridge in the distance. Hardly used the brakes on the bend in Kværndalen, I already had such speed that I floated up the hill, and hovered along the pallid yellow autumn-fields by Sand. My tongue was hard with breathlessness at the back of my mouth, down through my throat, down into my lungs. But I didn't think about the ride home, not for a second.

Gardermoveien had no pavement, just a raw road with deep ditch edges. Rough, worn tarmac.

I left my bike in the ditch, and stood on the top of my world, somewhere near Sand. Felt the demands of the task in the circus's categories. In the circus's company. My task alone and focused – a kind of picture. I had come so far in advance that it was up to me to fall back, regain an innocence, fall forwards in falling back – as though I didn't know what I knew, as though I stood at the back of the queue for knowledge about the world.

To cope with the independence and the juggler's tongue, warm, deep in my mouth.

And never say it.

It rained the whole autumn when the circus came, the ground was dark and wet, ripples of rhythmic, almost inaudible changes. The circus performers shook off the rain when they came in, got ready for departure, finished packing, had a cup of tea and left afterwards, before everything started. And no one waited for them more than a little girl with a red mouth who longed for another planet – this one – and who wanted to win a tightrope artist that didn't spit the act out again. She wanted to be taken on and won for her own tightrope act, from the inside, pierced by his on the outside, until everything was recreated in her again …

And that is how everything began, in a brilliant confusion of circus.

The field where the circus had been steamed by the sun. The black-trodden earth was edged with frost-cold yellow grass – sun-filled music in every blade for me, sun that lifted up the longing and the loneliness towards something else that must also have been there in the beginning. In the beginning of me. And I closed my eyes to the yellow grass in the sequins, the musical instruments, the make-up – and opened up the view. I built a city on the trampled-down yellow grass and the black earth. That was, I knew, how cities were built. Like Grandad's farm, Erling's flat. A kitchen table, cocoa and a cup of coffee. An open farmyard for free contemplation. A kitchen with warmth in the stove and a light on in the hall.

It was such a gift – such a compulsion, to be the sunshine.

And in the roughness of the circus's worn-out silk fingers and yellowing shadows, up towards madness, that's where it all came back to life.

I heard the music fade away each time it was said, and then resume resoundingly clear in my hard secret – becoming a definite demand through my muscles.

It was in my head, in subtle skewers. For tightrope artists, gymnasts – it's in their heads. Resounding in the animal tamer and lion juggling with each other's wounds – like the circus arena in the web of veins on a bloodleaf, when the circus had left me for the foreseeable future …

The tension in the drumsticks. The seconds clearly carved out. And something had to happen – like something always happens.

The big top was dimly lit, almost completely dark, just spotlights on the artists.

A man hung upside down from his knees on a swing, taking enormous swoops back and forth, back and forth, high above the circus ring in a deeply even rhythm. A woman stood on the other side, high up, grasped a swing in both hands, threw herself into the air, swung towards him – and let go. They grabbed each other when she was on the way down, precisely, right between fall and fall – a grip. And they threw themselves down into the safety net afterwards. Let themselves fall. Swung down into the ring. Reached out their arms. Reached out wide and received applause. Openly and generously, they received the admiration of the audience.

I didn't want to be a circus performer when I was older, it wasn't like that. I was one already. An open flight and a precise position in the very same cycle ride.

I haven't been to a circus since, but if feels like I have. My longing for the circus was perhaps even too strong for me to long for it, and for the circus to be enough. And since then I have sought out similar places – the smell of men and autumn, the comings and goings of roadside cafés and an audience's horrible laughter, the pure, masked force, the raw-carved precision. Another drink when it's all soon over again, beginning each time.

This is how I have borne the cut-off memory of what happened at the Jessheim Festival – a memory I have constantly had to confront, again and again. Far outside.

It was nearly dark when I cycled back from Sand. The sky was navy blue. The ground smelt faintly of premature, mustard-yellow decay. The sunlight shone horizontally across the fields, spreading a golden pink, reddish ocean over Romerike.

The fields sloped gently, the landscape opened wide, the sunset was a gateway to an even bigger opening – to embrace greater forces than there was room for at school, in Mum's flat, along the roads.

It was getting dark. I had begun on the long, hard hill up from Kværndalen to the motorway. The streetlights came on as I got off and wheeled my bike for a bit.

The roadside ditches were deep, pigeon-blue shadows that slowly sank into navy while I wheeled my bike past the community centre and the dairy.

They sat by the west wall of the dairy, smoking. I heard them before I saw them.

Now I see this as a potential turning point, having an eye for big headlines, dates, names and alliances. As if I don't know the person I was, but understood what was happening inside me at the time. (And I don't know who I am. I still don't know what it was that held me together ...)

It was Cecilie and two boys. One was dark-haired and massive, we were always afraid of him at primary school. He wore a leather jacket and had friendly eyes. The other one had long, wispy mouse-coloured hair. They were older than us. Cecilie was in class C at Allergot middle school.

Now they were on their way over to me. And now my heart is pounding. At the time I was calm.

It's Margrete from back then, who knows what will happen – and not me now, who of course knows. Now I can feel the tension I was such a part of back then that it was controlled and could be experienced as a kind of calm.

Controlled *because* I was part of it? I don't know. There are no reasons. That's how I was. There are only answers. As in *I know that* ... sentences from science lessons – *I know that* to control all that tension you must immerse yourself in it. Like you must immerse yourself in your opponent, either in his body or in his pulse, to get into position to fight yourself free ... To know your way free where there are only mute answers, obvious questions, blind insights.

They were going to go to a party, and wondered if I would like to join them. It felt like a kind of test.

The autumn chill was clear against the yellow streetlight glow. A shiny black, fluid clarity.

"Maybe," I said.

"Come on," said Cecilie.

So I did.

It was in the centre of town. The house was full of people much older than me. I stood watching them. Went from room to room. Sat on the floor and talked to the guy in charge of the record player. The music was good. Nothing was said. There were many faces I recognised. Some of them were nice but I was a complete outsider. In a way it was like an under-the-stairs place, yet not quite. It was possible to disappear there, just not if you were visible. You were left alone only if you became like them, it felt like. I cycled home.

I now think that I could have joined Cecilie's gang at the time. The way a mother would be scared, not knowing what her daughter was up to and fearful of the hard stare, the deep unrest, need to hit out, be free ... that's how I see the situation now and feel the teenager's longing, clearly desperate. Cecilie, who dropped out of school sometime in class 8 and was sent for treatment somewhere ...

At the time I was so independent that it makes me almost scream when I think of it now.

◊ ◊ ◊

"Would you like some?"

Erling looked straight at me. And he also saw me how I am now, as an adult.

"Yes."

"Yes, please," he corrected, kindly.

We sat in front of his TV having an evening snack. There was fatty pink Danish sausage. There was cocoa and milk. He had the balcony door open. It smelt of thick, fresh summer rain outside. Grit, the way it's hammered flat by chilly late summer rain.

His face was relaxed and focused – it held the world up. Every single expression on his face was in harmony with my breath, and unlike it – shaping my breath.

The room was dim with weak, warm evening light. And – there was something more than friendliness … the way there also was, but differently, in the face of the dark cheerful lady at "Fruity", who turned friendliness something else.

I don't know what it was.

"Fruity" – one of the wooden buildings in the main street, every sweet-toothed child's idea of heaven (until they closed it down when kids started stealing too much sometime in the eighties). It was a relatively small building, with two floors, divided in the middle by two wooden, glazed doors indicating the entrance. "Fruity" was through the door on the right. There was a counter in the corner at the back, a wooden hatch you could lift up to go in behind it, and loads of glass jars filled with sweets. On the floor there was a stand with big plastic containers on top of each other on a pole you could spin round, full of bags of sweets (that I couldn't afford). The ice cream counter was by the window. There was a display window. And the Easter egg I got from Grandad once when I was small, with dark pink tissue paper and yellow ribbon, that was from there – a treasure. And I was dark pink, deep yellow. A ray of pink sunshine. With the smell of marzipan and chocolate. Sweet and heavy. It meant a way of life. Not the egg itself, the colours and smell, but the way I owned it, how it was given to me – the me in those days, the colours cherished and conquered. And her smile, the lady with the black hair. Her dimples.

Once I was there with Kamilla without any money, and stood there pretending not to care, until in fact I really didn't want anything. *Don't feel like it*, I said. Waited for Kamilla to finish. *And one of those, and one of those, three of those ...* Dummies, sweet bananas, sour toads. And the black-haired lady patiently picked out the sweets and put them in the white cornet with gold patterns, looked me in the eye and smiled to show she understood. And then she winked and raised her eyebrows in the direction of the lollipops, seeming to say *But you'd like one of these, wouldn't you? Here you are.* And I got a toffee lollipop with chocolate coating.

It was all a contrast to the smell in the hall of the grocery store, which was a mixture of chicken wings, paint and sweets, and the way the other mothers looked at me. Because I was the one that always did the grocery shopping, as far back as I can remember, and I saw that they, either kindly or contemptuously, drew their own conclusions – about Mum.

The groceries were delivered to our door in big blue plastic boxes. In the end Mum didn't even write shopping lists, I knew exactly what we needed. And when the groceries came, I dragged the boxes through the doorway and into the kitchen and put everything away.

The dark-haired lady always stood behind the counter at "Fruity", she was the first thing you saw, the first I saw, when I went in. She had soft shiny skin, black velvety eyes, and dimples. She always smiled. Endlessly patient. She saw us. Gave the place a hint of the wider world ...

But there is still an extreme barrier – to saying what happened that night at the Jessheim Festival. Saying it is like making it real for the world. And it mustn't be real.

The muteness of the incident, like a silence to an inverse song (also from far away), this silence makes the memory new too, constantly reborn. And so the incident is real after all, as though – it's still possible to do something about it. It's still possible to keep what happened outside new rooms of reality … And it makes me stay young, with the possibility of continuing. It's as though – if I say it, I relinquish this weight that defines me, that keeps me soft and alive.

But I am still often afraid that the reality of what happened will entrap me. It's a feeling that *I know, only I know, I know how the world is, how people are* … And I get angry. Want to hit out. Knock down anyone that doesn't know, anyone that threatens me because they don't know, threatening my very existence because they don't know how the world is. Afraid I will suddenly knock them down, show them that force.

Saying it seems almost more impossible than repeating it …

The secret is a compelling muteness, a muteness to a song I always turn to, and in which the muteness turns into words only for me.

There was a song, and a fight, which I sang at the time without knowing.

There was an island. And a storm. It's that simple. And it started, and finished, that Saturday in August during the Jessheim Festival.

◊ ◊ ◊

So I had got into the cordoned off area for paying visitors, had sneaked in. Behind the town hall.

The earth at the funfair was trodden flat and black. It gave off a faint night damp. Dark damp. There was heavy August in the foliage, but on my bike – light, light speed, like a whisper through all the growth.

I floated and floated round and round the ring of raffle ticket stalls, fairground rides and closed market stalls. The funfair flashed with red and yellow and music, as if the music and light kept it all going.

I had a little money and walked around carefully considering what to spend it on. By the bumper cars I saw Sigurd and Lars from my class and immediately turned away.

They were the kind that looked right at people without knowing what they saw, and yet turned what they saw into something they could see. I certainly couldn't let them see me.

My heart was pounding loud and hard. And in those days I was slim, with thin skin, but my heart was tough and strong. It almost felt like my heart would beat its way out through my skin.

I turned around again, a bit further away.

The two from my class were each sitting in a bumper car, laughing wildly into the air.

Why was it so important that they didn't see me? It seems to be more than the fact I had sneaked in without paying. More than the fact I had lied to Kamilla. There was something about this feeling of being invisible, which had to be preserved at all costs. Almost as though I knew what would happen. As though it was me. As though I was navigating towards the one place I could get rid of this longing forever … wipe it out.

There was a faint, almost imperceptible breeze in the evening heat. Across an enormous distance the air was drawn to the rain that would fall the next day.

I didn't want to go up on any of the swinging, dazzling

rides. I just wanted to stay on the ground, be an invisible movement among all other movements. I just wanted to look, feel the night air, the music and the unfamiliar faces of the funfair. The dark faces that controlled the rides and swung around like in a dance (more than a dance), swung around between spinning, swinging teacups.

They barely kept their balance between slicing metal at speed. Rough metal against metal in motion, and black grease. Nearly like a train. A ship. A journey. Their precision was blind thuds in the stomach, from deep inside me.

And I looked them straight in the eye.

Those were the only eyes I looked straight into – strangers' eyes. Dark eyes that winked, smiled and saw right into the forces twelve-year-olds nurture like their precious young. This impulsive swaying, wavering of teenagers, which is also completely fearless – of slender limbs, with gleaming-brown summer skin. Nerves bared to each small breath of wind.

I bought a pink candyfloss. It was the first time I had eaten candyfloss. The taste was surprising, like fibreglass insulation melting sweetly in my mouth. A relief.

Then it occurred to me that an adult would soon spot me and ask if I wasn't too young to be out alone.

It shook me out of my consuming invisibility trance – an invisibility that allowed me to be all the more present.

And I was all the more invisible to others, unmovable in relation to their movements, no touching. All the more visible, instantly present, as if I was movable to myself. In the world. At one with it.

I could be all the more present when everyone was a stranger and no skin-intimacy revealed distances of suffocating dimensions. Skin-intimacy that led to intuitive withdrawals.

I had no sense that there was any difference between how I felt and how I looked. Never felt this distance many people talk about, between myself and the world. I was at one with it. Any distance was within me. But there was no distance unless I wanted there to be. There was no membrane. I was there. Reached out my hand and was there. Opened my mouth and the night air sucked itself into my blood, over my skin, over my face in a constant French kiss, the others' presence.

And I could leave, be somewhere completely different, somewhere unknown to others, and from there I could grasp back at the world …

And the mask I made for myself couldn't conceal anything, it had to be a mask of pure cuts and open wonder – because the way I touched the world, that was how the world touched me. Wasn't that also why I had to withdraw? Why all the horror had to be harnessed in a flight far into my solitude – like an invisible resonator for a face without pain?

In any case, I felt that no one saw me floating around at my own pace, where no one knew me and everything was foreign. There was room for me in the unrest. As if the unrest had already become the future and I had managed to erase it. As if I already existed on that star of the future I had decided to inhabit, and which I had located and was steered by.

I was on my way out the same way I had come in, where it was easiest to climb over the high fence, when one of the guards came walking towards me.

I turned around quickly, unseen, and darted behind one of the market stalls. There was a door that was open, and I sneaked inside.

And there he sat, in the makeshift back room. With a dirt floor. The Middle Ages, I have since thought to myself, it was a scene inserted from the Middle Ages. A war between something impossibly unyielding and me, my nothingness.

He sat in one of the closed market stalls furthest away from the crowds, furthest away from the fairground and the music on stage. He sat hidden behind a rail of clothes covered in plastic.

He sat there smoking, leant against the wall, with his elbows resting on his knees. Almost sprawling, relaxed. His head against the wall.

He saw little Margrete come in. And then he got up and saw her again.

She was about to turn back as soon as she realised there was someone there. But he grabbed her arm, grinned and whispered *No, come here. Come here.*

I can't remember his face and yet I can ... and sometimes I see faces that are different but the same; for example, when I wake up after a dream and for a few moments the face I remember from the dream is so distinct that my stomach contracts and I know, with a sudden jab of pain, what has happened, as if it's still happening. I can't remember which shop the clothes were from either. It smelt of chilled, thick plastic, away from the outside air. It was dark. The lights and sounds from the funfair seemed to come from far away. A distant sigh. Maybe it was children's clothing from *Peanuts*? Maybe it was *Twins*, or *Finn's Menswear*? Maybe *Nice and New* or *Jessheim Knits*? Or *Partner*?

But I will always remember the faint smell of alcohol on the breath in August.

Salty tanned skin. The smell of the sun's heat in soft white cotton.

Cigarette smoke in the night. Mildewed night air and alcohol.

I later remember all sorts of things that are easy and natural for me to know about. What happened doesn't belong to me. And yet it does. Little Margrete has carried it with her.

Carried it, almost like she – embraced it.

His hands, already a man's hands in a way. The black under his nails. The thick veins, bulging just under his suntanned skin.

The muscles under the thin, thin skin of a young man.

And he was strong, he was the first person I had met that made his strength visible – as intensely as I struggled in my life.

It was a survival instinct. I was broken. And I had to survive it. It was impossible to forget. And as it became such a defining moment, affecting every second afterwards, every breath, because it had become who I was, it could be remembered in a kind of deletion – as if the incident had gone inside itself. Inside of me.

That was the only way I could live with it. Because it was me. And I had to. And even though everything was different afterwards, I wasn't different. The world was the same. I had known that was how it was – and it was still me.

Yet it was impossible to know that was how the world was. No one should know.

I knew it for them.

And when I met Erling, I was blessed with a kind of certainty, I have since realised. Because he lifted up the incident, and my life, lifted the struggle that was my existence, which I fought with every fibre of my being to endure, without knowing that was what I was doing – he lifted it up when he saw me, embracing the knowledge of the world that I couldn't really know. Because he knew about what had happened, I was sure about that.

Only once did he ask me directly about what had happened that night. He had, of course, understood from earlier conversations.

"Erling, what do you do?"

I knew what he did, everyone talked about it, that he was a policeman.

He studied my face. We were sitting at his kitchen table having breakfast. He had found me asleep under the stairs again. He had been down to get the paper. He gave me cocoa and a slice of bread and butter and Danish sausage. Fatty pink sausage. Wonderfully different. And it felt disturbingly right to be there, with him.

"Well, Margrete," he said, "you know what happened at the Jessheim Festival, that's the sort of thing I work with, to find out about it. Find out what happened. The truth. People say so much that isn't true."

There was a hidden meaning to what he said, but he was clear all the same, questioning.

The night he found me under the stairs for the first time is imprinted in me. How I sat shaking far inside myself, recently showered and in clean, stiffly-dried clothes, tears as hard as bone. Ice-tears burnt into calm breathing and a wild, hard determination.

Now I acted as if nothing had happened. Looked right at him. My lying instinct was already well developed. But it wasn't a lie, pretending I knew nothing, it was beyond truthfulness and deceit. It was true – the necessary lie was silence, and the silence was true.

A survival logic.

"Do you know who did it?" I asked. "Is it true it was Ronny and his mates?"

Erling held my gaze, reflecting slightly too long. And I knew that he knew.

"No, it wasn't Ronny and Ståle. The police don't know who it was."

I don't know how he knew. And strictly speaking, I don't know that he knew. What happened also involved completely different incidents than the type of incidents people usually know about. And that can be told. People incidents …

And I am still afraid of aggression. My aggression. And the calm afterwards – when I cycled home, leant my bike carefully against the wall outside, went up all the stairs and let myself in. Showered away the blood. Rubbed and rubbed my skin sore. Cut my clothes into bits and threw them down the rubbish chute. Everything removed out of necessity, like an innate auto-pilot mechanism with disturbingly far-reaching dimensions. And the calm – when I had sat under the stairs for hours, days, afterwards, and could look Erling in the eye.

And then the late summer, the autumn with September rain, the circus the year after – the triumphs of the dwindling, yellowed light in me. The apparently naïve look in my eye.

"No, we probably won't ever find out what happened," said Erling. "We don't always find out, you know, Margrete. It's not always possible."

It was many months later, one and a half years later, when he asked me directly.

"Margrete, what actually happened at the Jessheim Festival?"

Out of the blue. I was watching TV and he was working at the table, reading some documents. It was a Saturday night. Mum was at work.

I was curled up on Erling's sofa with my knees against my chest, feet on the table. Eating crisps and drinking Solo and watching TV. It was the spring before Erling moved away from Jessheim again.

I didn't answer immediately. I kept watching, or rather, started staring at the screen. Took another crisp. Had to keep chewing slowly. It was many months later. One and a half years later, because I was wearing the blue wool jumper Mum gave me for my fourteenth birthday, when I was in class 8. It was in May or June 1977.

He sat opposite me, waiting.

And I knew what he was asking about. I knew that he knew, but I had never thought about it. The certainty had been blessedly mute. Like the weather. Like the shape of possible music between us. A kind of music.

"You know what happened," I said.

I kept staring at the screen while I answered.

"You know," I said.

"But Margrete ..."

"I'll tell you," I said, "some other time."

Afterwards I smiled as though nothing had been said. As though nothing had happened. When I smiled, I smiled like a middle-aged woman embracing the reality of the world, and at the same time I smiled the opposite, like an innocent child, because I was an innocent child. But all my joy was also a joy of knowledge about the force of the whole world and a flat-trodden joy at being able to live on the right side of this force. A joy at being able to live outside the reality of what had happened, and which had to remain absolutely secret. Even if everyone knew what had happened, I think to myself now. At the time, I was completely and utterly convinced that no one knew what had happened. It was in the papers. Everyone was talking about it. I knew *that*. But no one, absolutely no one, knew.

◊ ◊ ◊

I often sat behind the gym at Allergot middle school, behind the gym with the smokers, facing the woods. Many of them were from other classes, other places like Gystad and Algarheim and Sand, people I didn't hang out with in the afternoons. They were in the year above. Or else I might be with the solitary souls that stood far away from the cliques formed by emerging peer pressure and social class. With the slightly stooped-shouldered or angry, those with the wrong clothes and wan faces, from insomnia and all the strain. The closet-desperate. The closet-powerless. The stupid. But I didn't tie myself to anyone. I was friends with everyone and I was friends with no one, because I wasn't really friends with anyone at all.

I felt free at school. And my class was incredibly friendly. School was one big break time – or rather, more of a waiting room, like a waiting room at a railway station, and you could like the place for what it warned about and prepared you for, and therefore what it involved, but I looked forward to growing up. Being free. Even though everything was uncomplicated at school, nothing was required of me, I just had to be there, and do what I was supposed to. Sit and listen. Read and write. Apart from a number of social activities, like days out in the snow, the hassle of excursions (skiing in a queue), school was relaxed. Almost too relaxed.

The whole time I felt drawn to acknowledging the impossible incident that had happened. To repeating an equivalent release of force?

Once I sneaked into a nightclub with Lina and her brother and his friends. I was fourteen and you had to be eighteen to get in. I drank Coke and studied the awkwardness of longings and the enviable friendships from which these sprang. I danced a lot and laughed with them, because dancing was something I could share with them. I danced, drank Coke and looked forward to becoming an adult.

Afterwards one of Lina's brother's friends walked me home. He wasn't from Jessheim. He was tall and blond and I had a feeling in my stomach. We stood outside the entrance to my block of flats and he said *Bye then*, looking at me how I wanted him to. But he considered me a child all the same, and I felt the pressure building to grab him, I wanted to grab him, compel him, wanted him to take me, wanted to compel him – to be someone else. Erling … I felt the force of *Must, must,* and my chest tightened in a *Go, go*. With my stomach as hard as bone, jaws clenched and tongue thick in my throat, I ran up the stairs and straight indoors afterwards – after he had been *there* inside me, in my mouth, the wet skin of my longings, my force, where I was myself completely, with the force from the Jessheim Festival, so angry, so hurt … because he kissed me before he left, once, hard. Then he grinned. *Isn't that what you wanted?* And then he said *Bye then* again, softly, enjoying himself, and *See you* – before he went.

And I knew afterwards as I lay in bed. Knew the aggression was *there*, right there, in the same place he had been – against my lips, in my mouth, in trembling waves deep in my stomach, deep down in every fibre, nerve and thread … And I was furious. My longing was as desperate as my fear had been, it had the same force.

Sometimes I felt I had to break the pact and be with others that knew and needed external space for their rage. Others that hit out. That in various ways let themselves be hit. Maybe to make amends? To let it happen, like the final-decisive fear told them to? Let a man who was nearly, only nearly like him, for example, grip my wrists that way, nearly that way, as he had done … and let me delete it … and thus erase the incomprehensible fear of deletion and spiritual death.

But I never did, and the boundary between thoughts and action was established so very clearly, what it was possible to think and possible to do. And in the end it became natural, like breathing. That's how it was, like learning to ride a bike. Because you never forget where the boundary is. Never. Although the boundary is impossible to know about, an impossible pain …

The nightmares didn't start until some years later; I remember I found it puzzling that they suddenly appeared in my late teens. They have since come in phases. And it's become harder and harder to deal with them. As if they get stronger and clearer while the incident itself gets more and more distant, concerning someone completely different from me, the Margrete that doesn't exist anymore, but is still me.

I have always thought of Mum as silent and isolated from everyone else, everyone I spoke to, everyone at school, the teachers, the other parents, all the neighbours. She just came, and went. I picture her mostly on the sofa. Or with her outdoor clothes on, coat and handbag, in the car. Back and forth. I picture her mostly on the sofa with a magazine, hand-rolled cigarette and ashtray. The TV on. But I remember her talking to Erling one time.

They stood talking together in the car park for ages. Erling was about to leave and was standing by his car door. The pale blue Renault. Mum arrived. She stood there with her handbag over her arm, in her coat.

It was winter. Beneath the streetlights they were two adults talking together and I didn't know them. But it was Erling. It was Mum. And it must have contributed to the calm and naturalness of my being at his place, and in that sense the time spent with him was also a connection with Mum. In his jovial, outwardly-curious eyes – the way he looked straight at me, always laughing – in his easy manner with the world, there was Mum's possible, original concern for me. They spoke intimately. They spoke about me, about him keeping an eye on me. I know this from the odd word, gesture, look. How Erling said *It's my pleasure, Margrete, it's a pleasure for me to have company. And I've spoken to your mother.* And my world became bigger, so much bigger.

But I just keep repeating – that I died that time, and that when Erling lifted me up in the night, frozen stiff with essential isolation, a fossil of a child, he gave me new life. And when he glanced under the stairs and invited me to go up with him the following nights, or mornings, all that autumn, every time he did so, got me home and into bed, got me inside and off to school, he gave me the vital spoonfuls of meals and kind words other children were nourished with. And I was an infant. And I was ageless. Couldn't move. And I was twelve, had to get up and go to school, play a part in a play I didn't like, but that I had to make mine, make it possible to like.

I often wonder if Erling asked the paper boy to chuck the newspapers downstairs in the beginning, so that it seemed coincidental that he had to come all the way down, to get the paper, and then he found me under the stairs, and took me back up.

He didn't ask what had happened, when he glanced under the stairs and found me there the first time. He just said *Hi there*, and stood looking at me for a moment before he said *Come on*, and lifted me up.

As a student, I once worked at a psychiatric treatment centre for children and teenagers. I was twenty. It was the first time, as an adult, I began to have to deal with the present day of what had happened that night in Jessheim.

One of the girls at the home was completely *closed up*. Something had obviously happened to her, no one knew what. It was the usual thing. And they wanted her to talk, they thought that was her problem, that she couldn't *talk* about it. It led to endless conflicts, about everything. She was furious, about everything. And of course she in no way wanted to *open up,* the psychiatrist's unspoken password.

I felt that she had already been cut open. Somehow or other. And I also got angry, one day in the break room when they were talking about her as if she was a case, represented a group, a type of person. Fucking racists, I thought to myself. Her soul as they saw it was stretched out on polystyrene in the break room – disgraceful. None of her important personality traits or abilities were seen, I felt; there was no admiration, no respect. No laughter. And they stood ready with a knife to meet her hard stare, her terrified wide-open eyes. Her wings loosened and fastened in their conversations about her, in me, fastened by their thoughts, their power. And it pained me. Just like the threat that night in Jessheim … of being cut open. (And worse still – being cut open with sex, becoming part of another person where you are most your own, with the possibility of life, most on the boundary ... the final constraint, an unending death. The absolutely impossible, the thing that cannot happen. The thing I knew must not happen. Always knew it, long before his hand grabbed inside me, and his body softened just a second, and I bit him ...)

"Why is it so important that she opens up?" I screamed.

They just stared at me. There were three of them. A social worker and another student and someone else. They stared at me as if they saw the annoying first year student that I was, who had asked such a hopelessly basic question that they were incapable of answering it; and not from ill will or condescension, the distance was simply so great that they didn't know how to do it. I wasn't even studying psychology or social work. And there wasn't time either, to give me an introduction to universal truths before the end of our break.

I was heading into a rage.

"Why can't you just leave her be? Aren't you're supposed to be helping her? Isn't that the whole point?"

"Maaargreeete."

He said it slowly in a *There, there, don't get involved in things you don't understand, what's up with you anyway?* voice. And I suddenly felt my hand had stiffened in an extreme grip around my mug of coffee. I observed it. First with the wonder of an outside perspective. Then with impotence. I observed those white knuckles. Those blue-green veins. Time quivering with rage and without apparent reason in a blinding haze of warmth, beyond my control.

Suddenly all the strength in my hand seemed to vanish. I stared at the orange and brown striped acrylic curtains. I was losing hold of the mug, as if I had no muscles left. And that made me even more furious. I managed to concentrate the feeling back into my arm and threw the mug with tremendous force against the wall behind them. It shattered, with coffee and sharp pieces of china spraying back at us.

I never went back there. They didn't call. I didn't call. I have never seen them again. But I think they were right – they just didn't know about Erling's way of talking to me … keeping quiet. Moving silently to the place where you in silence reach sentences so complex that they cover secret incidents, and more than that – cover this nothingness I can't explain, but which keeps me alive, which exists in the odd word, all words, takes action.

I would often sit by the window in my room looking down at the car park when I was young, sitting so people couldn't see me. I saw when Erling came home. He would look up and wave. It was entirely good. Close, so that everything separated and became clear. And the world was big, wide, unending. As it should be. When he looked up and waved. The fact *that* he looked up and waved.

When I met Johanne again as an adult, we talked about waving from windows. It was one of the first things we talked about when we met each other as adults – because I remember so well the time when I was going to start dance class with her.

I didn't actually go there very long, to dance class. I couldn't bring myself to get ready. There was something insurmountable about it, too much of an effort. Everyone had a clean skirt and blouse, and nylon tights. They had special dancing shoes. They had an invisible hand to hold, which they could also let go of. They had to keep an eye on the time. It was in a shiny hall with music. A fairy tale castle. Turid Ramstad's School of Dance. They came and held dance classes once a week at Herredshuset, a large red wooden municipal building with a spire. There was a big hall with parquet flooring, long corridors and wide staircases to run up and down while we waited for the class to begin. And everything dance class entailed was presaged by the amber and black shadows of the huge maple trees along Gotaasalléen, which we went up to get there. It was a different world. An open devotion – an exertion of conspicuousness.

And then the thing was that Johanne's mother always waved from the window, gave her the bag with her shoes in, gave her a hug and told her *Come straight home*. Smiled. *Have fun!*

The thing was that I didn't fit in; I had this force that needed the balance of dance class so much that the longing for it, the passion, burst out with obvious clarity. It was *too* scary.

I recognised the summer night and music in August – and I owned that force, not the other way round. And it was dangerous.

I stiffened when it was soon time to leave. Couldn't move. Just sat glued to the armchair in front of the telly. Or if I was out, it was even more of an effort to go home, get my dance shoes and everything – and I sat under the stairs instead. Where Erling would find me. (Perhaps he checked every time he came home. And every morning. Thought about me every single evening, every morning.)

What we talked about, Johanne and I, as adults, and what first made me laugh and then almost cry, was that when her mother had stood in the window waving, I thought there was something she wanted to say, that Johanne had forgotten something or other, and I would stop and tell her that her mother wanted to say something. But Johanne just smiled and waved back. And she noticed my confusion.

"She always waves," she said simply.

And Johanne said that her mother had stood in the kitchen window waving goodbye every single day of school and dance class for twelve years, every single one. And it brought tears to my eyes, hearing that her mother had done that, and feeling Erling's arms lift me up the stairs in our block of flats.

I was twenty-one, and I was moved. Johanne noticed and said, not to comfort me, she just said it, *Margrete, it's fine. You're far ahead of me. I'm not moved by anything yet.*

I have never told Johanne what happened, even though we have that kind of intimacy, even though she's the one I talk to the most, even though she's my closest friend. I haven't told anyone (not even my husband, Halvor). But I think they know – that something like that has happened to me. And *that* has been enough, so far. Or rather, anything else has not been possible.

My intimacy with Erling is of another kind, it's vaguer, more basic, also less obvious – and I have promised to tell him. And it's exactly as if the promise has been brewing all this time, sometimes as a burden, a pressure and a weight, because it hasn't been possible to keep the promise, and the weight of that knowledge has been painful. Other times it has been more like a promise of relief. A necessary destiny.

◊ ◊ ◊

Recalling Mum's heaviness today, her heaviness from back then, also feels impossible. It's like a spiritual parallel to the Idi Amin dream – impossible to think about. It was as if her direction in the world was blind and distorted and constantly rejected. Never embraced, never seen. Never accepted or used. Never resting in wide-open landscapes …

There was a kind of inward energy – until a black hole appeared in her pupils, and she could only see the world through the eyes of her wishes. Looking into her eyes was like vanishing into a fairy tale, just much scarier. And much scarier now as an adult, without the blind seeing drive of a child, without the hope – knowing you'll be older, *Keep going, keep going*, knowing that *I must, I will*. I would grow up, I would get my own house, choose my own eyes. Then I would also be able to see Mum's eyes with all their heaviness, all their dread, and be free of them.

But it's almost scarier now, without an open future, without the natural hope of a child. Now I must know it all the way through, bear it for the child I once was. The child that I am.

I often tried to think about how it had got like that, why Mum was how she was, what had happened. Or if something had happened. Or if she simply was like that. And there was a whole load of questions that entailed a whole load of possible answers, and some of them involved Grandad's farm, the fields – autumn-empty, winter-stiff, snow-covered blue – against a foreground of multiple longings without a face. The bus that rarely came. The winding roads to get to town … Some of the answers involved whoever my father was, a familiar stranger. Familiar and a stranger, just as I was a familiar stranger too. A complete stranger, but a constant reminder by my very existence. Something about my eyes, about my forehead, that was unlike Mum.

The circus set free all such reflections and made them possible. Made me possible. Made a warm hand real, who I was. The magnificence of the circus, with golden teardrops shimmering in every blink – in a vision that was mine, but which still belonged to others.

And no incidents were ordinary for me as I split them into new ones with my eyes, threw up suns by the thousands, let them fall back bleeding to the ground – and was my own safety net.

There was a flood, an abyss, a quiet reflection. A withdrawal to the pulse of silence between me and the world. Exactly where everything just was – and I constantly came into being.

And I was the one who was thrown up, who landed whole, almost luminous ...

The day after the circus left I came cycling back from Sand. I cycled where the circus had been, under the big top and along the yellow wilting fields, the black earth. Around the circus ring, where flying from one to the other the ugliest became the loveliest. Where there was knowledge of the impossible in the artists' conviction of their ability to do it – the almost impossible flight, their precision being a matter of life and death – cascading over the audience. A cascade of brilliant, tender handshakes.

I was inexorably free there.

I sat at the side of the road in wet yellow grass, waiting for the circus and knowing that my tears were endless, without time and space. If I started to cry, I would never stop.

The impossible feeling had taken over me and I had to face the future with an iron will, for example in the form of a job, a house, a husband who would conquer me where I would conquer his conquest, where neither of us would die from it, but the conquest and the yielding light must be covered up and witnessed in a white shirt, mouth shut, and red lipstick, maybe.

The stronger I was, the further I could fall.

The more tears I kept inside, the more space I would put

between my tears and myself. So that one day I could drip a tear here and there, eyes closed, on lonely nights and nights spent under a man's skin, in public, at work, working – so the tears wouldn't tear me apart, wouldn't chase others away.

The weaker I was where the incident had left its mark, where I had let it happen, where I was still normal, the stronger I was.

The risk of falling led to this devotion to cycling at night, floating around, keeping watch under the stairs, future lovers.

It didn't cost less than everything else.

The whole of me was gripped in that struggle, and only then could I make it.

I stood strong amid the catastrophe in my midst. The connection of the highest waves with the stillest waters, burst into the structure of a single tear. This is what crying is. What is pressed out in the balance between me and the world.

The catastrophe is avoided in the shaping of the catastrophe – a dimension that can't be jeopardised, or calculated.

The rise in the circus ring's hard-trodden passage to China and my laughter in Grandad's fields were like a faint trembling of his hands – and he has held my hand all these years, the years since his death until now, and across all the fields, hills and roads to town, through all the seasons and landscapes – to protect me from myself.

The circus performers always came the same way, always in my possibilities of beauty – a way of looking at things.

The visible-invisible. The outside-inside, out again. Elephants, jugglers, trapeze artists.

I realised that Mum was broken, but in a different way, in a different place from me. I think I thought of her as, or rather, I considered her to be completely unlike me, almost like another kind of being. But then I was so obviously like her to look at, and there's something about looks that is more than magical. And not just in the eyes that see. The way she quickly turned her head towards the hall to listen, *Margrete, are you home?* As though she had suddenly thought of something – there was something she had to say. A jab in the stomach, as though there was something terribly important she had forgotten. That vigilance. Like mine.

There is at any rate something about looks that is decisive, and my obvious similarity with Mum gave my days a direction – my interest in the world had a tension. A force fettered in itself, between my family and Mum and me, inside me. A springboard. Her heaviness, her sourness, her silence and sighs were like an extra gravitation that made my direction in the world, my light-footedness, a necessity. An extreme balance.

We were both a constant fall in my limbs. I was a bow taut with power – over my bike, feet, speed.

I won.

There was a kind of elasticity, a necessity, that tied me to her mute demands for survival. And it tied her efforts to survive to my hasty exits, my proficient loneliness of incisive reflection and ample embrace.

There was a compulsion inside her, I felt, like an invisible, consumptive disease, that led to her unintentional moans and groans, her noisy silence. Like Åsa in my class, with a constant sigh on her smiling face.

Every now and then Åsa's sigh would come to the surface – *Ow, ugh, no* – but in her case the sighs began with a smile. In

Mum's case, there was a defiant, self-centred rejection, I have felt, a rejection and a demand for help from others.

When the teachers at school told us about Åsa's illness, told us she had leukaemia and was going to die, told us there was nothing else the doctors could do, and that it was a disease people died of, then I remember that it sort of happened again, what happened at the Jessheim Festival, but as if I was the one that was killed. It was as if the aggression had suddenly been directed at me, as if *that* was the punishment – to always have the shock inside me, like a fresh, constant cut. Always gushing with blood from soft, thin summer skin – and yet whole. Having to be whole, the whole time with my whole self.

I was dead, but had to keep moving. I continued breathing, moving, against all the odds. I was dead and alive in the same jab. The person from the Jessheim Festival was the same Margrete, the same dead Margrete, but always with fresh blood to feel the cut. The iron taste of fear in my mouth. Sticky-congealed blood smelling of Lano soap in the bathtub afterwards. (I still can't bear the smell of Lano, the smell of blood in soap bubbles …)

Åsa's illness meant she moved more slowly than the rest of us, awkwardly, and she easily got tired. Sighed. Groaned. Smiled.

I was one of the girls that used to walk her home when she couldn't face being at school anymore. It gave me a wonderful feeling of freedom and calm, leaving school with Åsa, and maybe Kamilla or Johanne. And we had to walk slowly, as she was so weak. She stopped and couldn't go on. Stopped and stamped her feet, like an overgrown child, a child that grew weaker the more she grew. Her long back, stooped. Big seeing eyes that knew that everything she saw would soon disappear.

And she was so weary, so tired. *No! I can't go on. I just can't.* And we would take her by the arm, one on each side of her – *No, no, no* – encouraging her, distracting her, until she giggled. *I know, I'm acting like a kid.*

I remember her having a smile that obviously cost her a lot, and hurt. She made such an effort. I need to concentrate to remember seeing her serious or cross, because she always had this disarming smile, always. But she was often fed up. And laughed at herself. Cried, and smiled.

We wandered up Cathinka Guldbergs vei, along the bridge over the motorway, where we would stand for a while, maybe, at the top, watching the cars rush past below us in both directions. In opposite directions at the same time. Like that game when you pat your thighs back and forth in opposite directions, up and down. That feeling of automatic control when you managed to do it fast. Or like putting your hand on someone's hand, then your hand again, fast, fast, fast, taking turns, in automatic harmony.

It was spring. Stiff birch twigs bursting green at the side of the road, in people's gardens. Heavy, black snow – the smell of warmth in water. Being outside.

And Johanne and I would walk back the same way afterwards, just as slowly, even though we didn't need to.

It was summer when Åsa died. All around the church it was green. Big, swaying birch gusts of green wind covered the cemetery, moving the world forwards. Bringing Åsa's frail smile to us.

I was accused of coldness. When Åsa died and I was the only one at my table (but not the only girl in the class) that didn't cry, they said I was cold and unfeeling. It was the first time I consciously realised that there's something inside, something outside and something somewhere else completely. I had a distinct feeling of being attacked by the power of conforming to norms. My first conscious experience of peer-tyranny. The fear of loneliness and exclusion. It was the first time I knew with words that on the outside all children are the same, but inside they're different. And you can cry or not cry, and it doesn't need to mean a thing. You can have friends and more friends, and there are different kinds of companionship. There are places for being visible and places for being clear. There are open companionships and there are confined rooms, where forms of action are limited to a stiff, slow death.

When Åsa died, I don't think I understood what it meant that she was dead. Even less than with Grandad. But I knew a long, long way inside, on the outside edge of my skin. That he was gone.

And perhaps you're supposed to learn how to cry in public? Does collective crying socialise us to understand the absence of the dead? What it means that someone's died? I don't know.

Åsa was no longer in pain, we knew that. We talked about it. There was so much she had dreaded. She knew life was a burden she didn't have the strength to bear. She was in peace.

But you're *supposed* to cry when someone dies. Somewhere inside. Like rain. Now I cry for the Margrete who died, or who never had life, who will always have certain forces distorted inside her, a crooked fracture. I cry for me. And in relief at being able to cry – and that crying no longer threatens to unravel into further crying, and further anger and crying – unravelling the whole world.

◊ ◊ ◊

It goes fast, incredibly fast. It has to. Little Margrete is contorted with fear turned to pure force. She kicks and bites and hits.

He's gaining control, holding her, he's inside her, or so it feels – for she is her whole self, her whole skin, all the way out to the tips of her fingers.

But he still only has his hand between her legs, he's reached the softest skin, and when he thinks he's in control, and relaxes slightly, just slightly, about to change his grip, Margrete bites his ear.

He drops the knife.

I don't know how he had been holding it, where it came from, I don't know if he was still holding it. It seemed like he had a lot of arms.

The flick knife falls to the ground. And Margrete wriggles loose, snatches the knife, and is about to leave with it.

And when he grabs her again as she is about to leave – this grasp around her wrist again, a handcuff – she turns round and lashes out, she's got to make him go away, got to escape.

The impulse lies at the bottom of my lungs like a constant pressure, ready to surge upwards when things are tough. When I'm hard-pressed or scared, I become little Margrete again, and feel the root of my tongue swell with the sensation of *Go away, go away*. Until I'm almost suffocated, everything freezes and almost nothing helps …

I don't think little Margrete knew she had the knife in her hand when she turned round and lashed out at him. I don't think she was aware of anything other than the blood-taste of fear (and of having bitten her tongue?). And the pressure in her lungs. The almost suffocating strain in her chest, which in the hours afterwards was a constant, stagnant thud that constricted her throat and turned her stomach to stone – until Erling demanded a smile and, like a hypnotist snapping his fingers, made the incident disappear.

Like turning a dial, Erling turned the incident inwards into Margrete until it was nearly all gone. Till it had become something else, a memory of another kind of time.

Her arms are extremely strong, connected to her whole back, stomach, the strength in her legs. She lashes out again and again. Stands so firmly that she has the whole weight of the world rising up through her body. The force with which she is holding the knife has one speed – like standing up cycling, a tension between the handlebars and throat, straight strong arms, long neck, raised chin, the speed of wind rushing over her face, her hair blown aside … And she must keep her balance, she mustn't fall …

She lashes out again.

Little Margrete doesn't really register anything until he falls. She's just a pressure of fear and an instinct telling her to run.

She doesn't know she has the knife in her hand until he falls and she feels something wet. Blood. She doesn't remember the actual stabs. Not really. Not the actual piercing of skin … She remembers the pressure of tremendous determination – *I must, I must* – and the wetness afterwards. Then she remembers the sight of him, his neck open, red, shapeless. Him falling. But she doesn't know if she remembers it.

And it wasn't blind panic either, and if it was blind panic, it's as though the grasp and the hard stare before and after the incident itself turned panic into precise intent.

Margrete stood there, a stiff tremor, staring at him.

He lay on the ground. Twisted. A heap.

And if he moved, she didn't notice. She stood there looking

at him, felt another jab in her stomach, and knew it would stay there unchanging and forever.

The moment little Margrete saw him, his neck slashed, the moments when the knife pierced skin returned to her.

The feeling that he and she were one and the same.

It was a clear and all-pervasive feeling that when she stabbed him, she stabbed herself. The feeling that she was slashed and dead. It was Margrete. The two of them were the same skin, the same blood. Her hands. His intent. But Margrete can't remember even as she remembers … she was no longer holding the knife. It must still be in him? She must have let go of it?

"The knife was still stuck in his throat!"

"How d'you know that?"

"He wasn't dead when they found him, you know. He had loads of blood pouring out of his mouth. Must have bled to death in the end …"

"Fucking hell!"

"Yeah, fucking hell."

"Nils's old man said he was dead as a doornail when they got to the hospital. And he's a *doctor*."

"Fucking hell, unbelievable."

"What a knife!"

"Bled to death. Fuck."

"Fucking sharp, those flick knives."

The teachers said there were a lot of things we didn't know for sure. That things like this hardly ever happened. That no one should be scared. And no one should be scared to speak up if they knew something. If anyone had seen something. And they said that people who did things like that, they needed help too.

Margrete doesn't really remember anything other than the pressure of fear and rage until she is on her bike, speeding down Gotaasalléen, towards the motorway. Home. She cycles standing up the whole way. Her chest is about to explode.

Everything else is conjured up, and even though the memory seems unreasonably clear, I know it can also be muddled with all the nightmares I have had as an adult, and all my thoughts.

Margrete's fear covered everything, making it clear and unclear at the same time.

I think that little Margrete was shaking so much that she couldn't move for a while, as she stood there looking at him lying on the ground, probably only a few seconds, maybe more, maybe less, maybe no time at all – before she wiped off the blood, her arms so incredibly strong again, she wiped off the blood, turned her T-shirt inside out and left. To cycle home.

She was shaking so much that she was completely calm, a single invisible movement going home, up to the flat and back down again, under the stairs.

I could have begun this by saying it was an accident. Self-defence. Insane at the time of the crime. But that's not how it feels. A survival instinct, self-preservation – certainly. But it's the aggression I remember most of all, and what I recognise. Again and again. The furious pressure. The automatic reactions – as if I knew exactly what I was doing.

And then that overwhelming calm of terrible necessity afterwards.

The killing left a sense of calm, this silent-mute knowledge that wasn't mine and was mine so deep inside that I had known exactly what I had to do when it happened. As if I had never done anything else.

It didn't leave a sense of unease, just a certitude, and an immense (almost violent) longing – for Erling.

Longing for a warm hand resting on my stomach as safely as a trapeze artist landing, without a net. As silently as breath howling after the stunt. As quietly as a hideous din to the human ear …

The circus performers come and go again, live on the road, construct vertically, high above the circus ring, in directions where laws are not written down, but kept in a stranglehold and loved in an embrace.

I sit for hours under the stairs, cycle around and around, sit in the dusk and concrete-cold listening to whispers between trailers and tents, along the road. Off I go, cycling further and further, in glimpses of raw force through soft, soft skin, in the artists' movements and mastery.

I study the movement that both cuts right in and becomes a grasp at the same moment, which isn't articulated, but which is spoken, encircled.

The elephants blink their small eyes – the show can now begin. They are adorned to breaking point, but balance their splendour precisely in their thick, grey-wrinkled skin – and spray the children's screams of delight straight back at them. Where the kids hold an eternity in each breath. A fresh fountain. That's where I take refuge.

◊ ◊ ◊

Today, I consider the way I was drawn from our flat to my place under the stairs and Erling's flat in light of my guilty conscience about Mum. Because I always had to go home again without wanting to. But I had to go home all the time – that was the place I should have been most attached to, and loved most.

And when Erling left, the day he left, I felt the burden of having seen him, of having known his flat, of having been held. The burden of having been able to love the silence under the stairs, of having absorbed the necessary distance. Secrecy's open channels for survival.

When Erling left, it also became clear that I had let Mum down, and that I didn't belong anywhere – nowhere else than with Mum, than with him, nowhere else than inside myself.

It has never again been such a long walk from the car park and up to the flat (not far at all) as the day Erling left and I said *Bye* and went back inside. Because then I had to take back our flat.

I suppose I survived because I had to. There's no other explanation for it, I just had to. I have sunk into the silence of all possible explanations.

The circus makes each silence significant, a self-control beyond what people outside the circus call unprecedented. A devotion in the heart of life, here and now. The audience can only sense this, dream about achieving this, when they lay the table, kiss goodnight, say hello – and *that* is the really dangerous stuff. A knowledge of freedom that the audience sense in themselves, in even the fleeting seconds of the magician's dexterity, in variations of truth and lies.

I sucked Love Hearts – pink, mint green and dry mimosa – while I raced around on my bike. I played "Love Hurts" again and again on Erling's tape recorder, the one he had left in my room without me realising it, and which I found when I came back up to my room after he had gone.

Love Hearts sang inside me while I cycled round and round.

My English wasn't good enough to know the difference between the song title and the sweets, but it didn't matter – I still knew. The demands of the world felt like a commandment: Thou shalt not love. I knew that breaking the commandment was the final rebellion. A wild triumph. Put up with the pain, use it, grasp it. Anticipate it – to let myself touch and be touched.

It was summer again and I knew as I raced down towards the blocks of flats that it's the stubbornness of silent-steadfast joys – *that's* what love is. *That* is the final rebellion. Love is the law that breaks all laws, it rises above all the crap and gives release. The law of the outlaws.

Now I can think this, maybe even believe it in a way. At the time I knew it with an assurance beyond anything I will ever feel again. Maybe not even when I die.

◊ ◊ ◊

I sat by the window in the flat. Cars came. Cars left. No one came. No one left. It was spring again. Drizzle. Acute, held-in tears about to burst through my skin.

If someone wanted me to come outside, I would pretend I had activities that prevented me from joining them.

I sat completely still by my window. Hidden. Inaccessible. I concealed all the truth and was true to the truth.

I was often ill when I wasn't. My teachers realised, I think, that I had to be alone sometimes. They made it normal. Made it okay. Maybe they knew what Mum was like. That I had taken the place of an adult. Maybe they had talked to her? In any case, they understood that it was best to give me time. It was no big deal. I could write my own sick notes. I got bad period pains and often stayed home. Even when I no longer got tummy aches when I had my period.

I sat quite still by the window looking out at the trees. Wind, rain, sun. Lay on the floor playing "The Boxer" and "Kathy's Song" again and again on my tape recorder. Sang and sang. Sat on my bed reading.

I read book after book. But none of the books I read at that time have stayed with me. I read anything that captured and created the world. There were a lot of spy novels, political thrillers, historical novels, whodunits. Vera Henriksen. Alistair MacLean, Frederick Forsyth. Agatha Christie, Georges Simenon. Even Nick Carter.

I was often angry with Erling in the years that followed, because he had let me love him.

It was a relief that he didn't come back to visit, that he never rang, or turned up. It would have been unbearable. And yet, even though I knew he wasn't coming back, I knew that he was alive, and I dreamt about him coming back. I lost myself in alternative worlds, creating rooms from his flat in my life, in our home. With me and Mum. The way he used to fling the duvet over the edge of the bed and air the room for hours – I did that too. I adopted the face he made when he observed the world with casual scepticism and friendly curiosity in his eyes. Clear, open eyes. And I soon became so good at it, or rather, I managed to make the rooms from my daydreams real – maybe I would buy a candle, like he did, buy the kind of bread he bought, say the kind of things he used to say, and I made it all mine, with my movements in tune with his. *Just look at that, Margrete. Okay, then.* His laughter. The way he laughed at everything. Lit candles. And I learnt how to make Christmas cake, like his mother had done that time I spent Christmas there.

I carved out a space for myself with a strength I didn't recognise then, but which was part of the force of fear and aggression. Which perhaps is the same force as the fatal-raw aggression, and which strangely enough seems to be the same force as the steady calm and playful joy of Erling's arms.

To lash out.

To let myself be touched with such poise that a new world cracks open each time.

I now believe he moved away because we'd become too close. Because I was no longer a child. Because I loved him too much and because he couldn't love me like that. Because he had made me his child, because he had given me life and held me like a baby in his arms, because he had not only seen, but created my beginnings, so he couldn't be a part of me like a boyfriend or a husband can. It would have been a kind of rape. But I love him even so, and he wasn't a father to me, I wasn't dead, I was a hundred years old, a fossil, twelve. But I know. I was twelve, thirteen, fourteen, and I loved him with the same force as I... as I lashed out with, and killed. The pure power in the split second, when time stands still, when you're the one holding the knife, in control.

And then this longing for resistance, for recognition...

Even so. What did it make me? Not a child. Not an adult. Not a daughter. Not a girlfriend.

I knew something that I shouldn't have known about the world. It made me a nobody in the world. And yet he took me and made me his friend. A friend in a world that couldn't go on. But which exists. Which is mine.

The autumn the circus comes – the autumn after – it pours down, and some of the circus performers say *That's it* and *Let's go for it.*

They play their cards.

No games or rules, just reality. They sing themselves drunk every night, with the circus lights, the circus rules – a secret about life lit like a full circle, a year for each second's burst and full intentions. Until the air in your skin thins out into tones.

You can work out the magic in the distance from the circus's hard facts, daylight, wrinkles, worn nylon and coarse, garish make-up to the refractions of light in the breastbone. You multiply the diameter by the concentration in little Margrete, who sits on the hard wooden bench forever afterwards. Where I sit on the edge of the road studying them. Where I cry dry sobs at night. Where I'm seduced from my seat in the audience, and where I am the star of the show. Where the dusk reveals the breastbone to show my face when encountering others – that is where I am.

Even hidden under the stairs I am so transparent that I have had to keep quiet all these years, not to destroy even more.

The mute lump of lead engulfing my throat cracks over the years, and spreads to rotting diamond-shaped growths on fingertips, irises, lips – it doesn't go away, cannot be separated from me, slicing me up more and more, until I have to speak up. Surrender it. Abandon it …

The slightest movement, the feather I am in the wind; the world skewers me and I slide through with my hands …

I gradually became so good at making a home for us after Erling left that it was often bloody awful how obviously small and empty our lives were, how out of place Mum was in the flat when I took charge.

White wood anemones in the grey afternoon light of the sitting room in May. No more than that. An impossible thing to ask of her.

When I wanted to cheer her up and she came home and didn't have the strength to be glad. That impotence faced with my aggression turned to open, upturned hands. That unruly balance – aggression's possible goodness.

Once I dreamt it was Mum I had killed. It was a strange dream. But I had come so far that I was in the process of denying her her refuge in the rejected, blind and emptied current of cold air where she could collapse, vanish alive – where she could settle down on the sofa, disappear from view, and just be.

I was in the process of making a home, breaking the ice, breaking the commandment.

And I cried every night for weeks the last spring I spent at home, because I knew I had to give it up, that I just had to leave, that I had stolen her defences from her, that I had no right to do so, that we mutually excluded each other.

I knew that the enormous effort it had required for her to keep me alive (with money, food, bikes and school things), the strength it had taken to maintain the façade, working and sleeping, sleeping and working, smoking and reading magazines, that effort was so vast that I couldn't even imagine it. Her force might seem to resemble mine, but it wasn't the same because she was broken in a different way from me, in a different place inside. Nor had her brokenness been embraced by another adult, not by her, not by anyone, and she didn't even live in defiance.

Did she live as if she were a child and just had to? A child with no strength, without time ahead, without certainty and hope? She had made up her mind, created a routine, and followed it. Whatever happened. Nothing else was possible for her. It was the only way she could survive, work, sleep, work, sleep. She gave me money for food, knew that I was there, went to school, managed. *Margrete, are you home? Margrete, I'm going now. Margrete, are you there? Is that you, Margrete?*

It was a part of her incredibly tough survival strategy that I should be okay. That was very clear to me. She never said so, but I knew I had to manage.

I believe that my actual survival after that night at the Jessheim Festival was pure luck – Erling was luck, my own childish strength was luck, pure chance. That's just how it was, how I was – and I knew that myself before I cycled up there that night and couldn't possibly have known what would happen.

But my survival still continues here and now, all the time – which certainly isn't luck, isn't a given, but maybe it's something I bring about? Something I allow to happen?

Once I dreamt it was her I killed, and it was as though I was Mum in the dream, I was the strength she lived off, and which took her own life. I was still the one that did it in the dream, I was her, but me. And I was the one that saw the huge effort it took to survive, I was the one that bore both the force and the gaze, like a knife.

She was broken even more deeply than me, I felt, the nights I lay there knowing I had to leave home.

Because I knew I wouldn't finish school in Jessheim. I would move. I would go to a school far, far away. I had to.

Mum didn't have a space inside where she could see her brokenness, I felt – see it both as if it were detached from her and inseparable, and then embrace it from a different place again. Embrace herself.

It was as though she were inaccessible to herself, and inaccessible to others – as though she couldn't … love. Not really.

But Mum could be loved, and that was what we both noticed when I started to take over and change things. I'd grown up so much, entered a new phase of life, survived and started to find a way forward. And it became impossible.

I loved her (I still do), yet I couldn't really love her. But I love her now, and I visit her once a week, at least.

I talk about my days, tell her about things I have done, seen, dinner parties I have been to, what we ate, tell her about trips I have taken, tell her about Halvor, about Johanne, other friends, about all the things I could have told her when I was a child, like other children do. I can see that she likes it.

Sometimes she tries to smile properly.

We are both child and mother for each other.

And I think she feels my gratitude – for never giving up, for helping us to make it.

Sometimes she looks me straight in the eye when I leave, wanting to reach out. And it's as if she knows that when I leave, when I get in the car and sit there quietly for a while before I drive away, that I always fight back the tears. Not sad, not glad. Because I can love. Because we made it.

Naked Eye Publishing
A fresh approach

Naked Eye Publishing is an independent not-for-profit micro-press intent on publishing quality poetry and literature, including in translation.

A particular focus is translation. We aim to take a midwife role in facilitating the translation of works that have until now been disregarded by English-language publishing. We will be happy if we function purely as an initial stepping-stone both for overlooked writers and first-time literary translators.

Each of us at Naked Eye is a volunteer, competent and professional in our work practice, and not intending to make a profit for the press. We see ourselves as part of the revolution in book publishing, embodying the newly levelled playing field, sidestepping the publishing establishment to produce beautiful books at an affordable price with writers gaining maximum benefit from sales.

nakedeyepublishing.co.uk

Lightning Source UK Ltd.
Milton Keynes UK
UKHW021838260522
403577UK00008B/1366